You Don't Have to Sit on the Floor

You Don't Have to Sit on the Floor

Making

Buddhism

part of

your

everyday

life

Jim Pym

Seastone

BERKELEY, CALIFORNIA

Published by Seastone, an imprint of Ulysses Press
        P.O. Box 3440
        Berkeley, CA 94703
        www.ulyssespress.com

First published in the United Kingdom by Rider, an imprint of Random House

Library of Congress Control Number: 2001094716
ISBN: 1-56975-304-0

Printed in Canada by Transcontinental Printing

10 9 8 7 6 5 4 3 2 1

Editorial and production staff: Claire Chun, Marin Van Young, Lily Chou, Lisa Kester
Design: Leslie Henriques
Cover Photography: SuperStock

Distributed in the United States by Publishers Group West and in Canada by Raincoast Books

To all my teachers,
and in particular to the memory of
Rev. Jack Austin
and
Roshi Tairyu Furukawa
with gratitude.

Contents

Preface ix

Acknowledgements xii

Introduction 1

The Way In

One Way In 10

The Three Jewels—Buddha, Dharma, Sangha 16

The Way

The Three Signs of Being 31

The Four Noble Truths 41

The Noble Eightfold Path 47

The Way Out

Mindfulness 57

Metta—Loving-Kindness 64

Meditation—East and West 70

Zen 75

The Koans of Life 81

Another Way—Pure Land Buddhism 88

The Eternal Feminine—Kwan Yin and Tara 96

Buddhism and Healing 104

The Circle of Compassion 112

Words of Power, Words of Peace 117

Rocking-Chair Meditation 123

The Way On

You Are Born Where You Are Born—
    Karma and Rebirth 129

But I Still Believe in God! 136

Buddhism and Prayer 143

Buddhism and Christianity 149

Buddhism F.O.C. (Free of Charge) 156

The Way Ahead

Let's Walk Together 165

Notes and References 169
Glossary 171
Bibliography 175
Useful Addresses 179
About the Author 185

Preface

◆

You don't have to sit on the floor to be a Buddhist. You can, of course, and millions of Buddhists do, but you don't have to. You don't have to learn Pali, Sanskrit, Chinese, Japanese or Tibetan (except perhaps for a few essential words). You don't have to wear any clothes that you would not normally wear, or eat any kind of special food. You don't have to attend a temple, or meditation group. You don't have to conduct or attend ceremonies or learn to bow or prostrate yourself. You don't have to study long and involved scriptures, or memorize endless lists. You don't have to chant, or do any kind of yogic exercises. You will probably have a shrine in your home, or at least a Buddha image, picture, or calligraphy, but even this is not essential. You don't even have to meditate! Yes, there are millions of Buddhists in the world who do not meditate.

You don't *have* to do any of these things, much less all of them. You can and should do those that appeal to you, or those that you feel will be helpful, but none of them is compulsory. Buddhism is far more than these external forms. I am not saying that these forms are unimportant, or denying that they have been found helpful to many Buddhists. I am affirming that they are not essential.

One of the reasons this book came to be written was a half-joking remark made by an educated friend who said, "I couldn't possibly be a Buddhist; I can't sit on the floor." This made me look again at Buddhism as I know it. I wanted to see how much is essential, and how much of it is the result of the everyday beliefs, culture and etiquette of countries such as Tibet, China, Thailand, Sri Lanka and Japan from which most of our teaching comes.

What is essential? The Buddha said that the Dharma was the essential thing. The Buddha was not a Buddhist. Buddhism emerged many years after the Buddha's death (or passing into *Parinirvana* as Buddhists call it) when his teaching became organized and split into factions, each emphasizing a part of the teaching. Yet even one of these is enough to lead us to enlightenment. The Dharma is the teaching of the Buddha, and it is the practice of Buddhism. It is also the experiences of millions of beings who, inspired by the Buddha, have achieved this state called Nirvana. We don't know what this actually is, but we do know that it inspires the life of one who has achieved it, so that they in turn become the inspiration for others.

I have been trying to live the Dharma for nearly forty years, and have come to the conclusion that it is truly universal. Wherever there are people who are seeking the way out of suffering, and are sharing it with those who want to find it, then the Dharma is there. Buddhism as a religion is still finding its feet in the West, and has received inspiration from many sources. We do not as yet have a truly British, European or American form of Buddhism, but the Dharma is living and can be found everywhere.

This book is not written to convert anyone to Buddhism, nor to encourage anyone to change their existing religion. It is about the essence of the Dharma, ways out of suffering. It is written from my own experience of where I have found it, and of what rings true to me. Most of the ideas have been found to be helpful in practice. There are also quotations, stories, visualizations and meditations, which are indented with a little symbol ❱ in front of them. They are intended for readers to reflect, contemplate or meditate on. I suggest they are read slowly, with a pause at the end. I have used them in this manner in retreats, conferences and workshops, as well as in other writings, and many people have commented that they find this approach helpful. I hope you will find it so, although I know that they will not speak to everyone. In practice, some people have found them interesting, but not right for them, while others have taken one or more ideas from the whole. This is as it should be.

If you find anything in this book that is helpful to you, then take it and use it. You are welcome to do this in whatever way you can. If not, then the book has some interesting stories and experiences, and I hope you will enjoy reading them anyway.

Acknowledgements

✦

There are many people who have touched my life, either through their presence or their words, without whom this book could not have been written. I am grateful to them all, and if I omit any from these acknowledgements it is because of my poor memory, and not through any lack of gratitude.

I have been lucky in my teachers. They have all freely given of their knowledge and being, but they are not responsible for what I have retained or practiced out of their teachings, nor of what is written here.

First, there was the unknown bikkhu who first expounded the *Kalama Sutra* to one who needed it like a desert wanderer needs water.

Then there was Sanuki, the former Zen monk with the wonderful sense of humor who taught a few friends out of compassion and fun. I never even knew his real name, but I owe him much.

Jack Austin, who elsewhere I have called "A Bridge-builder for the Light" gave me teaching, friendship and a share in his own Buddhist journey.

Rev. Hisao Inagaki, author, translator, sensei and friend, helped Jack and myself in our journey from Zen to Shin Buddhism. Zuiken (Rev. Saizo Inagaki) was Hisao's father, and also Jack's teacher.

Ling Chao, the "Shining Spirit" who has helped and inspired over many years.

Clare Cameron, author, poet and mystic, former editor of *The Middle Way* and *The Science of Thought Review*, was a spiritual mother to Beryl and me. She had fully integrated her Buddhism and Christianity, and helped me to do the same.

Max and Rosy Flisher have been friends and traveling companions on the Way. We have not always agreed, but friendship is more than agreement.

Roshi Tairyu Furukawa, Zen Roshi and Pure Land priest, taught by his being. His daughter Sayuri and his son Ryuji ably translated his teachings, and have also become dear friends.

Though I never met him, W. J. Gabb influenced my life immensely through his book *The Goose Is Out*. Other authors who have influenced me greatly are D. T. Suzuki, for just about everything he has written; R. J. Blyth for his understanding of the humor of enlightenment, and the Zen of European art, music and literature; and John Blofeld who shared the knowledge of Kwan Yin and Tara, and who was a master storyteller who both entertained and informed. They taught me much about Buddhism in its widest sense.

Then there are members of the Pure Land Buddhist Fellowship, The Buddhist Society London and the Religious Society of Friends (Quakers), all of who have given me "Sangha" in the fullest meaning of the word.

Ron Maddox, Secretary of the Buddhist Society, has been a good friend, and has encouraged me in my writing.

Judith Kendra at Rider has given me great encouragement. She has a great insight into the balance between what an author wants to say and what will appeal to readers.

Finally there is Beryl, my wife. When we met in our late teens I had already commenced an interest in Buddhism, and so in a way she has lived through the whole of my Buddhist experience, sharing it, yet remaining true to her own beliefs. She has supported me through all my writing, and I am so grateful.

To all those mentioned, and to many others who have touched my life but who are not included by name, I offer joined palms and gratitude.

I have used foreign words in the book as sparingly as possible, where there is really no alternative. They will be italicized when first used. I have chosen to use mainly the Sanskrit versions, as it is these that I am most familiar with. Occasionally, for example with the Three Signs of Being, I have used the Pali. There is a short Glossary at the end of the book that gives the various meanings and an indication of their importance within Buddhism today. The words karma, Zen, Dharma and Sutra have been imported into the English language (and can all be found in *The Shorter Oxford English Dictionary*) and so they are not italicized except as part of a title (e.g., *Kalama Sutra*).

Except where indicated, I have used my own versions of stories and quotations, which I have learned from various teachers and friends over the years. Versions of these stories have also appeared in a number of books, and I am unclear where I first read or heard them. Not being a scholar of languages, I must acknowledge the inspiration of various authors and translators, including D. T. Suzuki, Shunryu Suzuki, Paul Reps, Nyogen Senzaki, Anthony de Mello, Trevor Leggett, John Blofeld, R. H. Blyth, W. J. Gabb, Frederick Franck, Zuiken (Rev. Saizo Inagaki), Rev. Hisao Inagaki, F. L. Woodward, The Wheel Publishers and Peter Haskel. Full details of their works that have inspired me will be found in the Bibliography.

I am deeply grateful to these authors and their publishers for this inspiration, and apologize if I have quoted them without express permission. Thanks are also due to Zuiken, Roshi Furukawa, Sanuki and Ling Chao for their gifts of verses.

Without all those mentioned, and others who I may have forgotten—and to whom I apologize—this book could not have been written.

Introduction

✦

*By the Old River
A Tranquil Dragon,
and a Bridge-builder.*

—HENRYU

*I*f you go to almost any Buddhist center or temple in Europe or
the United States, you will find that the practice is mostly conducted sitting on the floor. You may find it very difficult to get a chair,
even if you are physically unable to get down onto a cushion. This is
just a symptom of the image that Buddhism has projected to the
general public. It is a direct result of everyday practice in Buddhist
temples in the East, and the expectations are those of the traditions
involved. Here in the West we have different traditions, and when we
go to church, many of us expect to sit on chairs or pews, and find it
easier to pray, meditate and relax if we are able to do so.

Similarly, much of Buddhist practice such as chanting is conducted in Asian and Indo-European languages such as Pali, Sanskrit,
Tibetan or Japanese, with no English translation available. If there is,
it is often poor, with little or no attention given to rhyme, meter or
actual meaning. Translation is often done directly from the diction-

ary, without reference to the fact that religious language is usually the language of poetry.

I remember attending the funeral of one of my teachers. It was conducted by a English monk of one of the Tibetan Buddhist traditions, and the chanting was beautifully done. However, the problem was that it was all in Tibetan, with no translation. As most of my teacher's relatives were not Buddhists, much of the significance was lost on them. I also have attended ordinations, funerals, weddings and naming ceremonies with Buddhist friends. Mostly the chanting was in another language, which, though beautiful for those who were familiar with it, was just confusing for the non-Buddhists present, even if an English translation was provided.

If I had been born anywhere in a Buddhist country in the last 2000 years I would have absorbed a Buddhist way of thinking and practice that would have been second nature to me. It would probably have included a variety of traditions, etiquette and superstitions, sustained by the example of my family, friends and co-religionists. Teaching would probably have come from my parents, visits to the temple, and from the Buddhist monastic order, the Sangha. Rites of passage would have been celebrated in a particular Buddhist way, and the whole would have been an integrated package, complete in itself.

However, I was born in the West in this modern age of virtually instant communication. Much of my early life was influenced by Christianity, and would have been even if I had grown up in a household that rejected it. Since learning of Buddhism, I have had access to books and teachers representing the whole spectrum of Buddhist thought and experience. Even when I chose a particular form of Buddhism, I was influenced by the practices of many other Buddhist traditions, to say nothing of other spiritual pathways. The same is true of many Westerners today who have either become Buddhists or are interested in the subject.

This can be wonderful, or it can be a disaster. I know from my own experience and that of others that the potential is tremendous, but creates its own difficulties. It is with this in mind that I venture to share some of the things I have learned. I am not enlightened. These are things I have learned from a variety of teachers that I have found helpful in making my life more harmonious than it would otherwise have been. I claim no authority other than that.

The majority of Buddhist teachers are Asian. I have had many such teachers myself, and I cannot say enough in gratitude to them. I probably would not be a Buddhist without them. However, I recognize—as many of them have done—that this can create a problem. With their teaching has come the etiquette, customs and occasionally superstitions that are a part of Buddhism in their country, and it is often difficult to separate the essential teaching and practices from these traditions. This creates corresponding expectations in Western disciples. The insightful teachers are those who teach the essential Dharma that is the Buddha's gift to suffering humanity, and leave us to work out the rest. They set us free, even to make our own mistakes, but are always there with help and advice when we need them (as we often do).

I am also grateful to have had Western teachers who understand the Dharma, the subtleties of the English language and the Christian-inspired culture that I have come from. This mix has provided me with what I feel is a balance in my understanding of Buddhism. Having received inspiration on my Buddhist journey from a number of traditions has helped me to be non-sectarian in my approach. I cannot claim to have experienced all forms of Buddhism, and I am sure that there are many that are equally as helpful as those of which I have written. They are, however, outside my experience.

I have written this book for people who are Buddhists, but have had problems with integrating their religion with their Western lifestyle. It is also for those with varying degrees of interest in Buddhism, but who have no intention of giving up their own religion (if they have one). This is quite in accord with the Dharma as I understand it. I became a Buddhist because my life led me in a certain direction, but I did not cease to love and respect the teaching of Jesus, even though I may not identify with all of Christianity. As far as I understand it, Buddhism—to say nothing of the Dharma—is about practice and not theory, and there is nothing wrong with people incorporating Buddhist practices into their own spiritual lives. I feel sure that the Buddha actually encouraged us to take whatever was helpful and practice it.

Another reason for writing this book had to do with reactions that I received to my two books on Quaker spirituality, both of which were written from the Buddhist viewpoint. In particular, there were letters and calls from people who had read *Listening to the Light*, saying that it had whetted their appetites to know more about Buddhist life, thought and practice. Was I going to write something similar on Buddhism?

In *Listening to the Light* I sought to give readers a taste of Quaker spirituality, and suggest things that they could practice within their own spiritual lives. I was not trying to convert anyone to Quakerism. This book has similar aims. I am certainly not trying to convert anyone to Buddhism, and I do not believe this is in the Buddhist spirit. I do recognize that some early Buddhists were missionaries, but the Buddha himself taught only those who wanted to listen. Buddhist teachings may cause some problems for those who already have a developed religion, but only if Buddhism is seen as a religion in opposition to other faiths. For me, it is not. Buddhist practice can co-exist with much of Christianity, for example, and actually does so in many ways today.

I personally know of many Christian priests and laity who practice meditation of various kinds that they have taken from Buddhist sources. This does not mean they have become Buddhists. There have even been a number priests and nuns who have become recognized as Zen Roshis or Masters. Writers such as Thomas Merton and William Johnston, while not receiving formal recognition, have been recognized by Buddhists as mystics and teachers.

The number of people involved in Buddhism in one way or another is growing. Many Buddhists are not linked with a particular tradition or teacher. Others find a home equally within Buddhism and Christianity. I remember attending a talk on Buddhism by a Catholic priest. At the end, he was asked if it was better to be a Buddhist or a Catholic. "Either," he answered, "but there is one thing better. It is to be both." If there had been priests like that around when I was young, I might never have left the Catholic Church.

Though many people live easily with the apparent contradictions caused by their position, some have difficulty in reconciling the two approaches. They do not look on Buddhism as a "rival religion," but appreciate its gift of ways through which they have been able to recover the deeper mystical side of their own faith. Yet still they feel the need to be able to justify their way of life to others. The injunctions of various priests and pastors—and even of some Buddhists—do not help.

I have been a Buddhist for nearly forty years, and have had my own personal struggles with these questions. Indeed, they still occur from time to time. Just as it seems I have found the answer, the question pops up again in a different form. I have been fortunate to meet a number of wonderful teachers—some personally, and some through their writings—who have helped me immensely. Many of them are named in the acknowledgements, and the stories of their contributions to my life and the lives of others are told in the relevant parts of the book. In my turn, I have also been privileged to be asked for help by many people who are going through similar problems. I hope I have been able to give it. What I have learned from listening to them has also helped me in writing this book. I hope that some of the stories might ring bells that will be helpful to those who read them.

Christianity also has much to give to Buddhism, and not only in the field of what might loosely be called "social service." Knowledge of the Dharma helped me to explore if it was to be found within Christianity. I discovered that there was a strong but little-known tradition of meditation within Christianity, and I have learned much from Christian writers and teachers that complements and enhances my Buddhist practice. Christianity has also encouraged Buddhists to become more aware of the needs of this suffering world, and to try to take care of them on a material level. A whole movement of what is called "Engaged Buddhism" has recently arisen, due in part to the influence of some Western Buddhists who recognized that serving those who are disadvantaged is also part of the Buddha teaching.

One of the great misapprehensions about Buddhism, which I shared in my early days as a Buddhist, is that Buddhists have to meditate. In one sense they do, but there is more to it than formal sitting meditation. There are many varieties of spiritual practice within Buddhism that are not called meditation, but which contain the elements that make meditation important. As well as looking at various kinds of formal meditation, I would like to highlight some of these other practices, which are all but ignored in most contemporary works on Buddhism.

Many people question whether Buddhism should be called a religion at all, but the fact remains that for millions of people it is. It is a religion, a philosophy, a psychology and a parapsychology, a metaphysical system and an ethical framework on which to base one's life. Most of all it is a Way. Though answers to most of life's questions can be found within Buddhism, the Buddha discouraged speculation. He encouraged us to find them by direct practice and experience. If we follow the Way, we can experience the same enlightened state that he found, and through this answers will come.

As Buddhism expanded and people came to experience enlightenment through their practice, their findings were added to the Buddha's teaching to make the rich tapestry of what we now call "Buddhism." Some of their ideas were put into the Buddha's mouth. Because there was no contemporary written record of what the Buddha actually taught, various schools sprang up, each teaching aspects that they considered most important.

The two main divisions became called the Mahayana and the Hinayana, or greater and lesser vehicles. There are many schools of the former still in existence, but the only surviving school of the Hinayana is called Theravada, or Teaching of the Elders. The term Hinayana is now considered pejorative, and seldom used. The Theravada retained the Pali scriptures, which were the records of the historical Shakyamuni Buddha's life and teaching. The Mahayana included them primarily in Sanskrit versions, but added many other teachings that were thought to have been revealed by the Buddha's mystical powers rather than actually spoken by him.

The other major difference is supposed to be between the Arahat of the Theravada and the Bodhisattva in the Mahayana teachings. I say supposed to be because I think it is more imagined than real. The Arahat is said to be concerned only about his or her own enlightenment, while a Bodhisattva refuses final enlightenment while there are still beings who are suffering. In fact, the Buddha refused to talk about the states of such beings. Personally, I do not believe that any enlightened being would so lack compassion as to be unconcerned while there are still beings who are suffering.

The very richness of the Buddhist tapestry can cause difficulties. It is hard for some people to accept that all these forms are from the same source. They feel that the original words of the Buddha as found in the Pali scriptures are enough, while others find their inspiration in one of the Mahayana scriptures or in the words of a particular teacher. Since leaving the church of my childhood, I have never

again become so deeply committed to one tradition or teacher that I
have shut out all others. I have had some teachers who are Buddhist
and others who are not. One of the fruits of this is that I find it easy
to celebrate with others when they have found the right way for them,
even if it is not Buddhist. I am sure that this is through the grace of
my teachers.

The Dharma is a Way that is as simple or as complex as you
wish to make it. It is like taking part in a treasure hunt. Each clue
may lead you on to the next, but there must come a time when you
stop and realize that you yourself must dig to find the treasure. I
have said it can be simple, but this does not mean easy. The Buddha
taught 84,000 different "Ways" to enlightenment to meet the needs
of many types of people. This is the Asian way of saying that there
is something for everyone. Dharma is almost anything you need it to
be. Anyone can find something within it that will fill a need. What
I wish to share is essentially simple. It does not involve a lot of learning, but it does involve some digging. Buddhism is essentially a Way
of harmonious living, or, as the Buddha said, "The Way out of suffering." The things I wish to share are those that have lessened the
suffering in my own life.

Bearing in mind what I have said about my gratitude to my
teachers, I will begin the book with the phrase that begins most of
the records of the Buddha's teachings. If I were truly honest and traditional every section would begin with this phrase that makes it
clear that the ideas are part of the oral tradition that goes back to
the Buddha. However, this would be tedious for the reader, and would
absolve me from responsibility for my statements. So, now, just once,
I will begin.

"Thus I have heard. . . ."

The Way In

One Way In

◆

For forty years
I have heard
Nothing.

—ADAPTED FROM A POEM BY ZUIKEN

There are several ways to start a book like this. I could start with the life of the Buddha and his basic teaching, but there are already many books that do this and do it well. I could also, if I had the knowledge, launch into deep Buddhist philosophy or psychology, but this book is not about such a way. This book is about *experience*, so the only way is to start at the beginning by sharing my experience of the discovery of the Dharma.

I first became interested in Buddhism by accident. At least, at the time I thought it was an accident. Now, after many years of treading my spiritual path, I no longer believe in such coincidences. There have been too many apparently chance incidents in my life which, with hindsight, constitute a pattern. The more I talk to other people about their spiritual journeys, whatever labels they wish to give them, the more I am convinced that coincidence is the label we give to such events when we do not see or understand their significance.

I was born and brought up a Roman Catholic, and had been destined to become a priest. However, by the time I reached fourteen, my mother was told that I should wait a while before committing myself as it was felt that I asked too many questions. My main problems related to faith, and to questions such as how a God of Love could possibly have allowed what seemed to me the barbaric sacrifice of His only son. I could not be involved in such an affair, and surely God was much more loving than I. Later, the full meaning of the story of the atonement was explained to me in a way that made sense, but at that time I could find no answers.

I left that church in my late teens, and become involved in left-wing politics and jazz. I was a founder member of the local Young Socialists, and one Saturday I went to a particular hall to attend one of their meetings. Unfortunately—or so it seemed at the time—I arrived on the wrong Saturday, and there was a meeting of the local Buddhist group in progress. I was a little late, but I was welcomed at the door and ushered in. Embarrassed, I tried to leave, but not wanting to disrupt the meeting further, and having nothing else to do, I sat down and listened to the talk. I did not realize it then, but this was a pivotal moment in my life.

The first thing I noticed about the speaker was his orange robes and his shaven head (rare in those days). I had not to my knowledge seen a Buddhist monk before, and this was another factor in my deciding to stay. I had missed the introduction, but he had just started to speak about something called the *Kalama Sutra*. The *Sutras* (Sutra is the Sanskrit term, also sometimes written in the Pali "Sutta") are the teachings of the Buddha. The *Kalama Sutra* is the teaching that the Buddha gave to the Kalama people. For me it was—and still is—one of the most important of all Buddhist teachings, for it solved the problem that I had over the question of "faith."

The Kalama Sutra

Representatives from the Kalama people came to see the Buddha, and asked about the various teachers who visited their town. Most of these teachers, having taught what they believed, reviled and pulled to pieces the doctrines of others. They were uncertain as to how to discover which of the teachers told the truth.

The Buddha starts by giving them the freedom to doubt and question, telling them:

> ▶ *It is proper for you, Kalamas, to doubt, to be uncertain; uncertainty has arisen in you as to what is doubtful.*

Then he tells them in a positive way:

> ▶ *Come, Kalamas! Do not go upon what has been acquired by repeated hearing; nor upon tradition; nor upon rumor; nor upon what is written in scripture; nor upon surmise; nor upon an axiom; nor upon specious reasoning; nor upon a bias towards a notion that has been pondered over; nor upon another's seeming ability; nor upon the consideration, "The monk is our teacher."*
> *Kalamas, when you yourselves know: these things are bad; these things are blamable; these things are censured by the wise; undertaken and observed, these things lead to harm and ill, abandon them.*

He then gives the positive aspects with the same reasoning:

> ▶ *If things are good, free from blame, endorsed by the wise . . . accept them.*

This was just what I had been needing to hear. Here was one of the world's great spiritual teachers (I knew that much about the Buddha) telling me that religion did not necessarily demand "faith," advising me to test things for myself, and to accept only those things that proved to be good and helpful. Its impact was as great as if I had heard the Buddha speaking to me personally. This feeling was so real that, to my shame, I cannot now remember the name of the monk who spoke.

There was—and is—much more to Buddhism than this. First of all, I needed answers to all the questions from my early religious experiences that had been buried under the surface. After the speaker had finished I went to speak to him, but he had to leave, and referred me to the chairman. He in turn called over some of the people present, and I remember quite a lively discussion. Though I do not remember the details, I must have received answers to my questions that satisfied me enough to set me on a course of study. Within the year, I had "taken refuge," and formally become a Buddhist. I also learned to meditate, but this came later.

Faith and Mystery

Even today the question of "faith" is still something that gives me trouble. There are many things that I believe; many people that I trust; and many things that I know through experience to be true. Whether any of these constitutes "faith" I do not know. The concept of "faith" does exist within Buddhism, but I have always assumed that this means trusting the words of the Buddha. The *Kalama Sutra* gives me the freedom to turn faith into knowledge and experience. Now, whenever I have this problem, I turn to the *Kalama Sutra* and it reminds me of the answer.

However, Buddhism is not without paradox and mystery. Although it was the logical and experiential aspect of Buddhism that first attracted me, all religions need their mysteries. There will always be mysteries in life, and religion without mystery is incomplete. Buddhism has its fair share, and I soon became attracted by the mysteries of Buddhism. I discovered that not only are things not always what they seem, but they are not always anything else either. Either, both or neither are accepted as true, and these apparent contradictions point to a realm beyond opposites.

One of my favorite Buddhist scriptures is called the *Hsin Hsin Ming* or *Heart-Mind Teaching*, and it tells us:

> ▶ *There is no difficulty about the Great Way*
> *Simply avoid choosing!*
> *When there is neither love nor hate*
> *It is there in all clearness.*
> *Deviate by even the thickness of a hair,*
> *And there is a deep gulf between heaven and earth.*
> *If you want the Truth*
> *Be neither for nor against.*

Another scripture, the *Diamond Sutra*, tells us that the Buddha is not to be recognized in a bodily form. Why?

> ▶ *Because according to the Buddha's teaching, a bodily form is not a bodily form. . . . All that has a form is an illusion, and the Buddha is only found when it is realized that form is no-form.*

I needed this as well as the logic of the *Kalama Sutra*. Such non-sense was for me not a question of faith. It was an instantaneous joy, something that made me laugh out loud and clap my hands. Not that I understood it with my mind; it all went deeper than that. The in-built humor was a release from the concept that religion needed to always be solemn, reverential and joyless. I was freed from the need to understand everything. It was my first insight into the joy of being able to say honestly, "I don't know," and this opened the way for all sorts of experiences.

This brings me to the subject of life and death. If you say that the connection is not immediately obvious, I would say that death is the great "don't know." It is also intimately linked with the development of compassion, which is the other essential aspect of the Dharma.

While writing this I have just had a telephone call from a very dear Buddhist friend to say that his wife has died recently. Here is the immediate impact of the real world onto an activity as nebulous as writing a book, and I need to find ways to deal with it. This book is about such "ways," so I follow the path of inspiration that emerges for me out of this otherwise sad news.

It has been said that compassion and wisdom constitute the whole of the Dharma. The compassion aspect of Buddhism was the final area that I had to experience, and this came though working with people who were suffering more than I was, in particular those who were bereaved. I do not have any final answers, but I did come to realize that compassion is probably the most important aspect of the Dharma.

The "Great Matter of Life and Death" is not only the concern of Buddhism. All the world's religions have sought to provide answers to a question that concerns every one of us. Fear of death is one of the great fears, and it is actually fear of the unknown. It is the final mystery, and although Buddhism provides a variety of answers, the Buddha himself was reluctant to discuss survival after death. As with everything else, his attitude was to help those who were suffering to find the way out. He knew that anything else would be subject to misinterpretation.

Other answers have evolved within the spectrum of Buddhist thought. There is a book called *The Tibetan Book of the Dead*, which provides detailed instructions for the person who is dying to help them adapt to their new life, and for those left behind so that they can help the one who has passed on. Some traditions, particularly in the Mahayana schools, speak of "Buddha Lands" where we can be reborn, and where there are no hindrances to our progress towards enlightenment. All this constituted a part of my search, until I came to realize for myself that the wisdom of the Dharma is not to speculate, but to tread the path to enlightenment, when, it is to be hoped, I will be able to understand free from illusions.

The Three Jewels—
Buddha, Dharma, Sangha

◆

Buddham Saranam Gacchami;
Dhammam Saranam Gacchami;
Sangham Saranam Gacchami.

I take refuge in the Buddha;
I take refuge in the Dharma;
I take refuge in the Sangha.

—*THE THREE REFUGES* IN PALI AND ENGLISH

The Buddha, the Dharma and the Sangha are known as the Three Jewels. In the simplest definition, the Buddha could be seen as the teacher, the Dharma as the teaching, and the Sangha as the community of monks. However, they are far more than this. They are the essentials in which Buddhists find their faith and practice.

Buddha

In spite of what you see when you look at most images of the Buddha, the Buddha is not Asian. The Buddhist scriptures tell us that there have been many Buddhas and other enlightened beings. The historical Buddha Shakyamuni was Indian, but nowhere does it state in the scriptures that only Asians can achieve Buddhahood. Yet this assumption is made by some people. In fact, Buddha belongs to all. Buddha is not Thai, Chinese, Japanese or Tibetan. Buddha is not male or female. Buddha is not human or animal, vegetable or mineral. Buddha is our Life, our Existence, our Mind, and that of all beings in any of the natural kingdoms, and even in worlds that we might not have discovered yet.

The word "Buddha" means a whole range of things to different people, even to the various types of Buddhists. It means the "Enlightened" or "Awakened" One, and is applied primarily to someone who has achieved the state of enlightenment through his own efforts. There have been many Buddhas, but the term "The Buddha" usually applies to Gautama the Buddha who lived in northern India some 2,500 years ago. He is also known as Shakyamuni, the Sage of the Shakyas.

The story of the historical Buddha is easy to find. However, one point to note is that the Buddha did not actually leave home to seek enlightenment. He had been shut away from the world, so did not know anything of the everyday troubles that beset us all. Then, one day, venturing outside as a young man at the height of his powers, he saw for the first time a man who was ill, an old man and a corpse. Once he realized that this was suffering, his natural compassion made him want to do something about it. He also saw a sadhu, or wandering holy man, who had given up everything to find spiritual truth. Gautama had an insight that this was the way to discover the causes of suffering, and the way out of it. He decided that he too would leave home. It was not for personal gain, but the search for a solution to sickness, old age and death that led him on the path to Buddhahood.

This is important, because there is a tendency among some Buddhists to emphasize the knowledge or wisdom aspect of the

Buddha's life and teaching. I have been told many times by Buddhists that the key factor in the Buddha's search was to acquire enlightened knowledge. Knowledge—or rather wisdom—is an important factor in the Buddha's teaching, but it is important only if it is motivated by compassion. Once the Buddha decided to share what he had found, he wandered around India with his companions for nearly sixty years. The Pali Canon or scriptures take place in the area of northern India and Kashmir, and tell of these wanderings and the teachings that he gave. They are said to be historical records remembered and passed on by those who were actually present.

The Sanskrit scriptures of the Mahayana show a different Buddha. They border on the mythological, and so teach in a different way. They are set on a cosmic stage, with audiences of millions of celestial Buddhas, Bodhisattvas (those who are enlightened but refuse to pass on from existence until all beings are freed from suffering) and others. Not content with teaching in a way that is pragmatic and down-to-earth, the Buddha of the Mahayana exhibits all the powers of a god, emitting lights, creating lands, appearing in different forms and being in two or more places at once. The whole is based on an infinitely vast conception of the cosmos that is beyond the ability of the ordinary mind to grasp. Time is expressed in billions of years, or in fractions of a micro-second, while other measurements are equally vast or minute. It is as if beings of enlightenment speak of things that can only be truly understood by other beings of enlightenment, and the message is that we are also enlightened beings here and now, but we do not realize it.

It is generally claimed that these Sutras were *revealed* by the Buddha through his samadhi, or deep meditation, rather than actually *spoken* by him. This does not mean that either one is more true than the other. It is accepted that there are different levels of truth that speak to different areas of the mind or manifest different aspects of reality.

A comparison between the Buddha of the Pali scriptures and the Buddha of the Mahayana might conclude that they are different beings. However, this would not be valid. The proof lies in the experience of millions of people that the teachings of both allow ordinary people to participate in Buddhist practice in ways that lead to enlightenment. In spite of the apparent differences, all of the Buddhist scriptures relate in some way to the historical Buddha, whether or not he ever physically spoke these teachings.

The Mahayana scriptures also feature many other Buddhas such as *Amitabha*, the Buddha of Infinite Light, *Bhaisajya Guru*, the Medicine Buddha, known as the Lord of Healing, and *Maitreya*, the Buddha to come. Maitreya does appear in the Pali Canon, where he is portrayed as waiting in one of the heavens from where he will become the next Buddha many years in the future.

Other sources claim that Maitreya has already been in incarnation. One form is so universal that he appears in many homes that know nothing of Buddhism, yet paradoxically so little is known about him that, apart from Chinese Buddhists, few know of the story of his life and enlightenment. This is *Pu T'ai* or *Mi Lo Fo*, the so-called "Laughing Buddha." He is portrayed as a fat and jolly figure, often carrying a hemp bag, and sometimes pictured with children climbing all over him. Few Buddhists actually know him as a Buddha, and I call him "the Buddha that nobody knows."

There is one other meaning of "Buddha" that is truly universal. This is the Buddha Mind or Buddha Nature, which is the true essence of all beings. This Buddha Mind is the mind we have from our birth, and even before our birth. It is the "Unborn" of which Shakyamuni Buddha speaks briefly in the Pali scriptures.

▶ *There is, oh Bikkhus, an Unborn, an Unmade, an Unmanifest and an Unbecome. If it were not so, then there would be no escape from the born, the made, the manifest and the become.*

The "Unborn" is often interpreted to mean the state of "Nirvana" or Enlightenment. This may be so, but as the Buddha refused to explain what Nirvana actually is, it is hard to know what he meant. However, there are many who will testify to the existence of this Buddha Nature. Because it is incapable of being grasped with the mind, it is also known as *Sunyata*, which translates as emptiness or the void, the state beyond and including Oneness.

> ❱ *When the Buddha achieved his enlightenment, a rain of flowers fell on him from the heavens.*
> *"What is this?" he asked.*
> *"This is in gratitude for your teaching on emptiness," said the gods.*
> *"But I have not yet spoken on emptiness," said the Buddha.*
> *"You have not spoken on emptiness; we have not heard emptiness; this is true emptiness," was the reply.*

Thus, the term Buddha may mean a number of things. However, whether we are talking about the historical Buddha, any of the cosmic Buddhas about which he taught us, or the Unborn Buddha Mind that is our own nature, we are actually talking about the same thing. In fact it is best not to talk about such things. As Shakyamuni taught us, speculation of this kind is fruitless unless we walk the Way and practice the Dharma in our everyday lives. Then all the apparent contradictions of the difference between mind and Mind, self and Self and all the knots and tangles caused by words will dissolve in the Deep Silence that is Buddha.

Dharma

The Buddha was not a Buddhist. He taught the Dharma. He sought to correct the religious teaching current in his day, and to add the insights of his enlightenment. Buddhism did not emerge until many years later. The Dharma is the Law, the way things are. It is the way of practice and not of theory and speculation. In spite of this, there has grown up a huge collection, both monastic and lay, of speculative and philosophical writing and commentaries on the rules of life. All this I call "Buddhology."

The Dharma is not exclusively Asian. It is Universal. It consists of those things that the Buddha discovered for himself, and is intensely practical. It contains a mixture of a profound ethical code and a "Way" to realize the nature of the self. It is found in various forms in most of the world's religions and spiritual teachings, as well as in art, poetry, music and works of compassion. The Dharma is essentially the law, the way things are in a well-ordered world, and, of course, "the Way out of suffering." The Hindu tradition has its own concept of Dharma. In fact, the name often given by Hindus to their tradition (of which the Buddha was a part) is *Sanatana Dharma*, the Eternal Religion.

Much of the Buddha's teaching was in response to the questioning of the Brahmins and others. It was not until about 350 years after the Buddha's death that his teaching was written down. The majority of what we call Buddha Dharma is teaching to those who were willing and able to leave home and family and devote all their time to the attainment of Nirvana. There is little instruction specifically for those who wish to devote their energies to the same goal within lay life. Indeed, many writers have speculated as to whether it is possible, and whether the Buddha thought it was possible. Some say that because the Buddha found it necessary to leave home to seek enlightenment, his message is that it is only possible to be enlightened if one is a monk. They say the best that lay people can hope for is to be reborn as a monk in the next life.

I do not think this is so. In fact, I will go so far as to say that if I believed this was the case, I would not be a Buddhist. I believe with all my heart that the Buddha did intend that his teaching could be understood and practiced by lay people as well as monks, but that the teaching and practice will be different. The Buddha did teach that lay people could become enlightened, and the experience of millions of Buddhists through the ages points to the same conclusion. Lay people do contribute to the general decrease and even annihilation of suffering in this world, but they do it in different ways. Lay and monastic Buddhist practitioners are both essential to the Dharma, and are complementary to each other.

The Dharma has been confused with meditation and similar practices, but it also includes the profound moral and ethical teaching that is contained in the Noble Eightfold Path, which we will consider in detail later. This ethical teaching of the Buddha is sometimes overlooked even by Buddhists. It was and is as important a part of the whole Dharma as any of the spiritual and mental exercises.

The Dharma is a whole. It is a Way of Life that is a complete map for the journey of life. The Buddha's approach is not the only one, and he never claimed that it was. We have seen how the *Kalama Sutra* puts the whole thing into perspective by relating it to personal experience. This even applies to those parts of the Mahayana teaching that are called the *prajnaparamita*—the "Perfection of Wisdom" or the "Wisdom Gone Beyond"—where the mind is taken beyond all form and concept to the realm of suchness or emptiness. Even here is the promise that it can be practiced and experienced.

When the Buddha was dying, he was asked what those remaining would do for a teacher. He told them, "The Dharma will be your teacher." He knew he had not written a book of the teachings, nor had they been recorded in writing at the time. I feel that he saw Dharma as a living entity, and not just a body of remembered teachings. It is also clear that he recognized that it would be subject to change as all things are. What we call the Buddha-Dharma today is all that the Buddha taught and revealed. It is also the total of the experiences of all whose insights and experiences make it a living tradition.

Sangha

Except perhaps in the very early days, Buddhism was never a single entity. Very soon after the death of the Buddha, the teaching started to break up into factions based on certain differences in belief and practice. Buddhism found particular forms in each country where it settled. There is a definite difference between Thai, Sri Lankan, Tibetan, Chinese and Japanese forms of Buddhism. There are also variations between—to take Japan as an example—the Tendai, Zen, Jodo and Nichiren schools, all of whom emphasize different aspects of the teaching, and base their practices on different scriptures. Nonetheless, wherever there is a community of people who are seeking to follow the Dharma, there is the Sangha.

The Sangha is usually regarded as the ordained community of robed monks and nuns. However, many people feel that this is a limited definition. Another way of looking at it is to say that the Sangha is, as one of my teachers put it, "The aggregate of all enlightened ones, and all seekers, in all times and all worlds." This widens the field considerably, and can include most of us.

One problem with saying that the Sangha consists only of ordained bikkhus is that the definition of "ordained" has changed considerably in the time since the Buddha initiated men (in the first instance) into the homeless life. In fact, the Buddha did not ordain anyone. He merely encouraged those who would follow him to embrace the homeless life, where their daily food was earned by begging, and their only "work" was meditating and possibly teaching lay people. Later these disciples began to organize and to build monasteries and other centers where they could live, while still going out on the alms-round to beg their food. As these centers grew in size and number, they became more and more powerful and some people believe aspects of the Buddha's teaching to lay people was lost.

There is a story about the Buddha and Mara. Mara is the Buddhist devil, and a real trickster character. At times he seems to be as enlightened as the Buddha, and to be helping him in his mission, while at other times he appears to oppose him.

> ▶ *The Buddha and Mara were standing together talking (as they often did). While they talked, they idly watched the people passing by.*
> *Suddenly, a man bent down and picked up something bright and shining.*
> *The Buddha turned to Mara, and said, "That man has found a fragment of truth. That ought to worry you."*
> *Mara laughed. "No," he replied, "You see, I'm going to help him organize it."*

The monasteries continued to grow. As Buddhism spread, it split into sects and factions, who, I am sad to say, did not always agree, and sometimes expressed that disagreement violently. Buddhism is often regarded as a peaceful religion. This is mostly true, but it has had its violent moments, usually over Buddhalogical speculation, the very thing that the Buddha had warned his followers not to indulge in.

As Buddhism extended to other countries, monasteries lost their characteristic of depending on the lay people for food and robes. There were some perfectly good reasons for this. Other countries were colder than India, did not have a tradition of holy begging, and had social structures that meant that the monks had to find other ways of living. This was all right provided they remembered what they were there for, which was to seek the way out of suffering for themselves and all beings. Too often they sought the short-term way out of suffering for themselves, building up riches much in the way that the medieval monasteries did in England, and with the wealth grew increasing power.

Some remembered the Buddha's teaching, even in the midst of a life that was very different from the Buddha's.

▶ *An arrogant man went to visit a well-known monastery. He came in the front gate, and passed an old monk sweeping leaves. He rushed past him, up the drive, and came to the front door, where he was welcomed by the guest master.*

"I need to see the senior monk on an urgent personal matter," he said.

The guest master nodded, and sent for the head monk.

"Are you the most senior monk?" the man asked.

"Oh no," said the head monk, "you need to see the abbot."

"Fetch him," said the visitor.

"I can't do that, but I can direct you to him, but you will need something to enable you to communicate with him," answered the head monk.

"OK," said the visitor impatiently, "let's do it."

The head monk handed him a broom, and led him outside.

There were also still a few who lived the homeless life. They were mostly hermits or solitary monks, and they usually continued the alms-round. They often countered their reputation for holiness with irrational behavior, aimed at discouraging visitors. Some were on friendly terms with the animals, even the more deadly varieties. One such monk was called Sukhananda.

▶ *Sukhananda lived in the jungle, where he spent his time meditating. His only company was the animals, and, by virtue of his meditation, he learned to speak to them, giving them advice and helping where possible. He felt this was his destiny. He only ventured into the village for food each morning. As he walked, he often found people in some kind of trouble, and these too he helped, offering such wise advice that he quickly became known as a saint.*

He worried about this, and discussed it with his animal friends when he came home, asking them what he should do about this increasing adulation.

One day, as he was about to set out on his daily alms-round, he found his path blocked by some monkeys, an elephant and a tiger. "What is wrong," he inquired. "Nothing," said the head monkey, "but we have come to help you, as you have helped us. We have brought you your food." So saying, the monkeys trouped by, each one dropping fruit and nuts into his bowl until it was full. Next came the elephant, who had stored up water in his trunk, and proceeded to fill his water pot.

Finally came the tiger, who said that he had not brought food, as he only ate meat, and knew that this would not be right for the monk. "I have come to ask you to preach the Dharma after you have finished your meal," he said. Meanwhile, the villagers missed Sukhananda and thought he had been killed. "It must have been that tiger we heard growling," they said. One woman, braver than the rest, suggested that they should go into the forest to find his body and give it a burial. "Though we do not know the rites, I am sure that the Buddha would accept our efforts," she said. But the others were afraid, and so she went off alone into the jungle.

Some way in, she heard a great cacophony of noise, with the sound of tigers, leopards, elephants, the squeal of monkeys and many other sounds that she did not recognize. She felt afraid. Turning a corner, she came on a clearing, and saw the monk sitting preaching to a vast circle of animals, all sitting in harmony with one another. She was too frightened to run and too fascinated to turn away.

The animals heard her, and turned towards her with a great noise, but the monk said a word, and they settled down. "Come," he said, "and hear the Dharma." She wandered into the circle, and was offered a space between a tiger and a huge monkey. There she sat, listening to the holy man, who told them of the Buddha, and of his love and compassion for all beings. As she sat there, she felt that it was the Buddha himself who was talking to her, and she felt a state of great wonder.

When the teaching was over, she asked the monk why he had not been into the village for food, and he told her all that had happened. "The trouble is, now," he said, "if you go back and tell them what you have seen, my reputation will grow even more, and the real glory is the Buddha's, not mine. What can I do?"

The woman asked if she could stay with the monk. "I am not allowed to consort with women while I wear the robes," he replied. "Then," she said, "here is a way out of your dilemma. Let me stay and be your disciple, and your reputation for holiness will disappear among the villagers. You can ordain me to the homeless life as the Buddha did, *we can both find peace for our meditation and preach the Dharma to the animals."*

And so it was!

The Sangha or Community is a vital part of the Three Jewels and, as with everything else, it is subject to change. Only those who could live the homeless life joined the Sangha of the Buddha's day, but today this might be almost impossible. In the modern Western world, most Buddhist monks and nuns live in communities. Buddhism here is just in the settling-in stage. It is not clear what form the Sangha will take for us in the future.

Because influences and teachings have come from a variety of traditions and countries, we do not have a coherent Western Sangha. Instead, we have a number of sanghas held together with the label "Buddhist." Many Buddhists are aware that we cannot afford sectarian strife. In order to avoid it we need to look to the essence of the Dharma to find what we have in common, rather than look at those ideas that divide us. Yet there is something more. One of the principal aspects of the homeless life is that of not being attached to people and things. If we can manage this where we are, and yet maintain compassionate friendliness to all beings, then we are living true Sangha.

These three, Buddha, Dharma and Sangha, constitute the basis of Buddhism. People who wish to formally become Buddhists "Take Refuge" in these three. Publicly they confirm their desire to become Buddhists by repeating the words with which this chapter started, and some Buddhists repeat them at the start of every *puja* or service, and at the beginning of every meditation session. The rest is up to them. In these ways they affirm that these three are indeed Jewels or Treasures beyond price.

The Way

The Three Signs of Being

✦

I enjoy the blossoming flowers
And the cold of the falling snow.
How deep is my joy
For all things as they are.

—TAIRYU FURUKAWA

One of the significant things about the Buddha is that he speaks of things as they are, and not as they should be. The Dharma commences with his discoveries about the nature of the world as it is, and allows us to take them as working hypotheses. From this point, we are encouraged to find out for ourselves whether what he said is true. It was this freedom that first attracted me to Buddhism. As described, my Buddhist voyage of discovery commenced with the *Kalama Sutra*, and the next stage was finding what are called the "Three Signs of Being." This is simply the nature of things as they are. "As they are" is not only the beginning of the Way, it is also the end. Over and over again within Buddhist teachings we are told that enlightenment is not a long way off, but right here in our natural state. The process of becoming enlightened is really nothing more than the process of remembering.

The Buddha said that there were three things that we needed to remember about every living being: they suffer (*dukkha*); they are constantly changing (*anicca*) and that their essence is "not self" (*anatta*). We are not meant to agree to these things just because the Buddha said them, nor to simply accept them with our minds. The purpose is to real-ize (my hyphen) them, that is, to make them a living reality in our lives. When we have done this, we may be enlightened, or "know."

Let us look at these points in detail, and see for ourselves if we can agree with them, and if they are true for us. Bear in mind that my explanations will not be completely satisfactory because I am not enlightened, and because I am writing them down, something even the Buddha did not do. Remember, as with all things, they are definitely subject to change.

Dukkha

Dukkha is often translated as "suffering." It does mean suffering in its widest sense, but it has also been translated as "ill," "evil," "restlessness," "unsatisfactoriness" and even dis-ease. Dukkha is the opposite of sukha (ease, happiness, peace and well-being). It is largely the effect of our reactions to change and our lack of understanding of the nature of the self. Dukkha, anicca and anatta are interdependent. Life is unsatisfactory because it is changing, and because our vision of who or what suffers is not clear. Dukkha is the result of living in this world of change.

This includes the obvious things such as birth, aging, sickness, dying, pain, affliction and despair. It also includes the fear of losing possessions, relationships and other things that give us happiness. Critics of the Buddha's teaching have accused him of being unnecessarily pessimistic. If he had left it there, it might be so. However, he did not only highlight the problem, but pointed out that there is a way of solving it for ever, and even gave us the details. No one can call that pessimistic.

◗ *Pause for a moment and watch your breath to calm the mind.
Don't try to change it; just watch it.*

*Now look at your own life.
Look carefully at your body (with eyes open).
Now become aware of your body, every part (with eyes closed).
Do you really like every part of your body?
Be aware of physical pains, aches, stiffness, tension and other
limitations.
How does this affect your view of your body?*

*Observe your thoughts and emotions,
How you react to the things that happen around you.
Consider your mind and thoughts, your fears, hates, resentments,
worries, impatience and other negative thoughts.
Is there anyone you resent or hate, or who makes you feel angry?
Be aware of your loves, joys, feelings of peace, contentment and feelings
of achievement.
Do you worry about losing these?*

*Look at your emotions.
See how they, whether positive or negative, can displace all your good
intentions and kind thoughts.
Do you feel guilty when they do?
Remember your principal actions over the past week.
How do you feel about them?
Do you feel any of the thoughts or emotions already mentioned?
Do you wish you could change any of them?
Do you wish you had done something that you did not do,
Or not done something you should have done?
How does this make you feel?*

*As you look honestly at your thoughts and emotions in this way, are
you aware of things that you wish to change?
Can you consciously change them?
If not, can you accept them?*

Or do you feel a restlessness, an underlying concern, a feeling that all is not satisfactory?
Can you understand that all this—and much more—is dukkha in your life?
Would you like to find a way out?
Read on!

Anicca

The second basis of existence is change. Everything changes, and keeps on changing. There is nothing in the world that is not subject to this law of change. Modern science has confirmed the Buddha's discovery. We now know scientifically that everything changes, and is changing all the time. The atomic structure of all created things is forever in motion, and so changing. This applies not only to the material world, but to the world of ideas and emotions.

The Buddha proposed the idea of change because it is obvious. It is obvious to anyone who pauses to look at it within their own lives. Movement, breathing, eating and drinking, digestion and excretion, thinking and feeling are all change. A similar exercise to the one above can be used to observe change.

▶ *Pause for a moment and watch your breath to calm the mind.*

Be aware of your body, every part (with eyes closed).
See how there is movement at all times.
See your breath, the rising and falling of your diaphragm.
Feel the movement of the breath in your body.
Be aware of physical pains, aches, stiffness, tension and other limitations.
See how there are slight movements to compensate for these.

Observe your thoughts and emotions,
See that thought is forever moving.
Consider your mind and thoughts, your fears, hates, resentments,
worries, impatience and other negative thoughts.

*Be aware of your loves, joys, feelings of peace, contentment and feelings
of achievement.*
See how all these are moving, changing, rising and falling.

Look at your emotions.
*See how they, whether positive or negative, can displace all your good
intentions and kind thoughts.*
Try to observe how they rise and fall away.
Do you want to change any of them yourself?
*Observe how, if you acknowledge them and leave them alone, they fall
away and settle on their own.*

Observe the world around you
And your reactions to it.
See how it and they are changing all the time.

*Do you feel a restlessness, an underlying concern, a feeling that all is
not satisfactory?*
Can you acknowledge this change as being an integral part of your life?
If you can, then relax, and read on.

Anatta

The final sign of being is the one that has caused more discussion and
controversy even among Buddhists than anything else. Anatta literally
means "not self" or "non-self." We cannot really experience it except
with an enlightened mind, and we do not really know what kind of
mind that is. What kind of mind is a mind without a sense of "self"?

In fact, we are asked to take anatta as a working hypothesis, and
observe the problems that are caused by considering ourselves as fixed,
unchanging, separate individuals. We are encouraged to see that such
individuals undergo suffering, and to see how everything changes in
ourselves and the world around us. Based on these observations, we
look at the Buddha's teaching as to what constitutes a "self," and see
if it presents a more reasonable possibility.

In order to begin this process, it is helpful to look at the usual meaning of "self." It is not a question that many people consider in the normal course of events. *The New Shorter Oxford English Dictionary* gives a number of definitions including, "the person in question"; "any of the various conflicting personalities conceived of as coexisting within a single person" and "a person's nature, character, considered as different at different times." These definitions indicate that, even within ordinary English usage, the self is not necessarily fixed and unchanging.

Another definition is "true or intrinsic identity, personal identity, ego." Here we come closer to the idea of "soul" in various religions. The *Dictionary* quotes the philosopher A. J. Ayer as saying, presumably with reference to life after death, that which is supposed to survive is not the empirical self, but the soul. So here we have a question. Did the Buddha intend anatta to refer to the self or the soul, or were they considered the same in the India of the Buddha's time? Maybe he was referring to something completely different? There are many theories, but I am not sure anyone really knows the answer.

I think that what the Buddha was arguing against was the brahminical theory of *atman* or soul. In this, the soul was seen as a spiritual entity in opposition to both body and mind, appearing as a miniature god-form living in a cave within the heart of the worshipper. The Buddha, being essentially pragmatic, could see how much these views would confuse people. He also had an insight of his own as to what constitutes a human being.

Once he had fully seen the universal nature of change, the Buddha knew that living beings could not be an exception to this rule. In his enlightened state, he looked at his own nature, and saw that it was composed of five ever-changing elements, which he called *skandhas*, meaning heaps or aggregates. These are form or body, feelings or emotions, perceptions or imagination, impressions or intentions, and awareness or consciousness. They are essentially empty, forever changing and subject to suffering. They constantly interact with each other, and each contributes to our state of being at any moment. Their relative strengths at the time of death determines our rebirth. The skandhas are one of the principal reasons why the Buddhist approach to self is different. They are the essence of the Buddha's views on the self. Once we grasp this aspect of his teaching, we gain a great insight into our being, and particularly the way in which we display a variety of "selves" to meet differing circumstances.

On occasions, the Buddha kept a "Noble Silence" when asked about the self. Other Buddhist masters have used different methods.

> ▶ *A fisherman came to a teacher, and asked, "What is the nature of the self?"*
>
> *"A puff of wind in your net," replied the master.*
>
> *The monastery cook heard of this, and asked the same question. "The hole in the middle of your noodles," was the reply.*
>
> *A learned monk, who had been studying scriptures in the same monastery, came forward and asked, "Why don't you give them proper answers?"*
>
> *The master got up from his seat, and invited the monk to sit there. He did so.*
>
> *"Are you comfortable?" asked the master.*
>
> *"Yes, thank you," said the monk, adjusting his robes.*
>
> *"Then," said the master, "You tell us, what is the nature of the self?"*
>
> *The monk started to reply, but the master hit him with his staff.*
>
> *It is said that the monk was enlightened.*

Such stories help us to look at the Buddha's teaching on the self in a new way. It does not matter whether he was saying that there is a self, or there is not a self. Both are just concepts, and we no longer have to speculate. Instead, anatta is seen in its true light as meaning something that is neither self and no-self, and both, and between and beyond the pairs of opposites. It is beyond all our concepts and ideas. It is almost as if we can hear the Buddha saying, "Nothing you can say about a self is right. Don't bother! Live the Dharma, and walk the Way."

As we begin to try to discover these things for ourselves, we have to act as if we were a "self," and inquire as to the nature of that self. As we look ever deeper and get glimpses of the truth, we become more reluctant to put it into thoughts or concepts, let alone words. Maybe it is not possible to be totally self-less while we are un-enlightened, as while we are seeking for enlightenment there is always *someone* who is doing so. This is why some contemporary teachers emphasize that enlightenment is "nothing special" or just "being ourselves." I remember the shock the first time I was told this, as I had always thought of enlightenment as being something very special.

Let us investigate who or what we really are.

▶ *Who am I? What am I?*

Think about the nature of the self for a moment.
See once again the changing nature of all that you can observe.
Is there anything that is unchanging?
Who am I? What am I?

Sometimes our bodily form is most important.
Can you remember a time when this was so?
What did you do to enhance the impact made by your bodily form?
How did this change the total you?
Who am I? What am I?
Sometimes your feelings or emotions are the most important.
Remember a time when this was so.
How did they affect your attitude?
How did they affect your body?
Who am I? What am I?

Sometimes it is not the emotions, but the way you see them.
Can you remember a time when this was so?

Are you aware of the difference between your actual feelings and the
way you perceive them?
Think about this for a moment.
Who am I? What am I?

Sometimes it is your reaction to things that determines what happens.
It has been said that most of the time we do not act; we re-act.
Is this true for you?
Our reactions come from outer forms, from feelings, from perceptions.
Look and see if this is true for you.
Who am I? What am I?

How have these four impinged upon your consciousness?
See how your consciousness of life is shaped by form, feelings, percep-
tions and reactions.
Yet there is something that includes and contains them all.
Have you ever been aware of the way your consciousness functions?
Like all the others, it is constantly changing, but this changing is
consciousness itself.
Who am I? What am I?

Look clearly and see how your form influences that which you call
yourself,
And enables you to think and act as if you were a self
Though a self that changes according to action.
Who am I? What am I?

Now do the same for your feelings, the way you feel things,
And for your perceptions, the way you see things,
And for your sensations, the way you experience things,
And for your consciousness, the total of them all.
And continue the questioning,
Who am I? What am I?

Who am I? What am I?
Listen!

There may be no answer in words,
The answer may be in the Silence;
The answer may be in the question;
Who am I? What am I?

Can you see that dukkha, annica and anatta are not just theories? They are facts that we can, even in our unenlightened state, see for ourselves. In the seeing, something changes. Our view of life becomes re-oriented, and we get a glimpse of what the Buddha meant. However, it is vital that we do not make the mistake of replacing our concept of "self" with a concept of "non-self," for then we are back in the world of duality.

Maybe this was what the Buddha was trying to tell us when he claimed to be "awake," and encouraged all of us to "wake up!" He would not have done this if he felt that it was beyond our capacity to do so. We do not have to do anything special except remember. Then all will become clear.

The Four Noble Truths

◆

If you see Truth
With limited wisdom
You see only its shadow.

—ZUIKEN

*M*y introduction to Buddhism through the *Kalama Sutra* and the Three Signs proved to be right for me. It gave me the basis from which I could understand the path that the Buddha taught, and I very soon became convinced that it was the right way for me. My problems with faith meant that I needed to have a very firm foundation of understanding before I could commit myself. It seemed that things came in the right order for this to happen, and I wanted to learn more. It was time for me to be introduced to the Path.

I wish that those who recorded the Buddha's teachings had found another way to do it. The teachings were not written down, and were remembered in two ways, both of which cause me problems. The first was poetic form, and much of the Buddha's teaching is put into verses that summarize the teachings. The poetic form is one of the classical ways of remembering stories, and it was highly developed in the India of the Buddha's day. However, it does involve a great deal of repetition.

The other way of remembering facts is to compose lists. I remember His Holiness the Dalai Lama saying at one of his general talks that Buddhism might well appear to non-Buddhists to be a religion of lists. Personally, I find these endless lists to be one of the least attractive features of Buddhism, probably because I have difficulty in remembering them. For others, they are most helpful. I try to use the minimum number of lists, and only list those things that are essential. The Four Noble Truths and the Noble Eightfold Path are essential. They were the basis of the Buddha's whole teaching, and the content of his first sermon. So let us start with the First Noble Truth.

The Truth of Suffering

The first of these truths is the Truth of Suffering. We have already looked at this in some depth. It had a tremendous impact on me when I first heard of it. I had been suffering from depression, and was going through a difficult time, not been helped by well-meaning friends who were involved in spiritual teachings that emphasized positive thinking. I tried positive thinking until it felt as if my head was being bashed against a brick wall. In a word, it did not help. So when I read that the Buddha had said that "life was suffering," I felt another instinctive leap of recognition.

Even in the state I was in, I knew that there were happy times. What about those? The Buddha did not deny that there were happy times. He emphasized that both happy and sad times come to an end, and that we suffer by worrying about what we might lose or gain. Suffering is the starting point, and the springboard from which we dive into the Dharma. Once we have decided to dive, we cease to worry about the board. If suffering had been the whole story, my interest might have wavered. However, the Buddha also claimed to know the cause, and that there was a way out. He taught that way. As a result of hearing this teaching and practicing the Path, others had also found the way out of suffering. This was what I needed—and still do need—to know.

The Cause of Suffering

The Second Noble Truth asks, "Where does this suffering come from? Why is it that, overall, our lives are unsatisfactory?" The Buddha said that all suffering comes from "grasping," "craving" and "desire." We crave sensations of various kinds, and, if they are pleasurable, we crave their repetition. We grasp what is pleasant, and try to escape what is unpleasant. We desire our individuality, to be born again after we die, or to survive in some heavenly world. If we think we are likely to go to hell—particularly if that hell is eternal— we may even long for extinction. When we are somewhere, we want to be somewhere else. When we have friends, companions, lovers, we try to find others. "The grass that is always greener" is a perfect description of the desire that brings suffering.

One of my teachers used to say that even the desire for enlightenment is a barrier to our ever finding it. Certainly, among Buddhists, the constant search for perfection causes what he used to call "seeking sickness." We look here and there, read this and that, go to hear the latest teacher, yet all the time what we are seeking is right here. "You are what you are seeking" is a sublime truth. The teaching of the Buddha is that enlightenment is to be found here and now, and we do not have to search for it. Jesus said the same thing when he told us that the Kingdom of Heaven is within us.[1] Bankei Zenji, the famous seventeenth-century Zen master, pointed out that the faculty that enables us to distinguish bird-song or identify the sound of a drum, and that we have received from our parents, is none other than the enlightened Buddha-Mind.

Looking at our own lives, we can see there is a problem. We have been taught from childhood that it is good to have ambition, to seek to improve ourselves and the world, and to help those whose suffering is greater than ours. Did the Buddha really mean that we should not seek to improve ourselves and try to make the world a better place? I do not believe that he did. In the Second Noble Truth he is talking about desire to possess, which comes from our concept of self, and not that which flows from true compassion. Letting go of self and all that it involves allows wisdom and compassion to flow out into the world, not in the way that we desire, but in ways that are in accord with the Dharma.

From this development of compassionate action wisdom evolves. Our automatic reaction when we discover something wrong is to do something about it. This is good, but can be based on desire. If we have developed wisdom and compassion, we are enabled to act rightly and in ways that are without self and without the desire that creates more suffering. If we honestly recognize our own lack, then there are always others who might see potential in us.

▶ *There was a worthless son of a great lord who was unable to find anything to do in the world. His father sent him to a monastery where he studied for many years, but his mind was not on it, and he regularly used to escape into the town to sample its pleasures.*

Eventually, the wise abbot called the man to see him. "Is there anything you are good at, apart from drinking, gambling and cavorting with the town girls?" he asked. "Well," said the young man after some thought, "I am quite good at chess." The abbot sighed. "Come back and see me in an hour," he said. The young man went away and returned in an hour, to find a chess board set up, and an old monk sitting beside it. The abbot was also there, cradling a large sword.

"You will play a game of chess," commanded the abbot. "This monk is quite good, and has sworn obedience to me. If you win, I will chop off his head, and he will go to the Pure Land, from where he will certainly be enlightened. On the other hand, if you lose, it will be your head that is forfeit."

The two men sat down and began to play. They were evenly matched, but eventually the old monk made a mistake, and the young man began to press his advantage. His concentration was very deep, but in one of the pauses, he took time to look at the old monk. He saw, as if for the first time, a man who had not merely studied Buddhism, but had given his life to achieve enlightenment for the sake of the world. The young man saw in the monk's eyes wisdom and compassion, and he began to look at his own worthless life in comparison. Awareness of the abbot with his big sword made him sweat, but he reached out and made a deliberate mistake.

There was a crash as the abbot cut the board in half with his sword, scattering the pieces in all directions. "Enough," he cried, "There is no winner and no loser." Turning to the young man, he said, "To walk the Buddha's Way, two things are necessary, awareness and compassion. Today you have shown both. Stay with us, and I know that you will make progress."

It is said that the young man later became a famous Buddhist master with many enlightened pupils.

The Ceasing of Suffering

The Third Noble Truth is that of the ceasing of suffering. The Buddha was perfectly clear at all times that suffering can cease, and that this possibility is available to all. His whole teaching led up to this point, and even the next step was designed to bring it about. The way is very simple—though not easy. It is to go beyond all this craving by discovering the true nature of the self. This is the way to let go of all that creates suffering, and to do so in a way that no longer creates causes of suffering.

If he had left it there, it would be a great insight into life, but not very helpful. But the Buddha was not one to leave his teaching half finished. He knew that this simple approach was not for all, that the many types of human beings would need different techniques. So he taught the Dharma, and its many ways of practice. However, we do not have to know them all. We have only to find those that are helpful to us. The Buddha tried to make it easy by condensing 84,000 down to eight, and this is the Fourth Noble Truth. It is called The Noble Eightfold Path, and is the subject of the next chapter.

The Noble Eightfold Path

◆

Do not just tread
The path of the ancients.
Seek what they sought.

—BASHO

The teaching that the Buddha called the Noble Eightfold Path is to me one of the clearest and most detailed expositions of the spiritual life that has ever been given. It includes ethical, moral and mystical guidance. Because it is written as a sequence, some commentators have thought that it is a graduated path, with the final step of meditation more important than the first one, our view of the world. In fact, it is a unity, and is only presented in list form for convenience. I remember being told of an elderly woman who had been a Buddhist for most of her eighty years. She could not remember the details, and called the whole Path, "Right Everything." I have often felt that she must have been well on the way to enlightenment.

The Noble Eightfold Path consists of eight practices that are designated "Right":

- *Right view (understanding; attitude)*
- *Right aim (intention; resolve; aspiration; motive or thought)*
- *Right speech*
- *Right action (or conduct)*
- *Right livelihood (means of living)*
- *Right effort*
- *Right mindfulness (awareness)*
- *Right contemplation (meditation; concentration)*

There are some variations in translation, but the Pali term *samma* does mean "Right." It also means supreme, highest or perfect.

Here we have the whole of the spiritual life. The Noble Eight-fold Path is the teaching that is absolutely essential for the understanding of Buddhism. It includes all that we have spoken of so far, and much more besides. It covers the ethical, moral and spiritual understandings of the Buddha's teaching of "The Way Out of Suffering." All three aspects are of equal importance, and have to be practiced simultaneously. Practicing any one to the exclusion of any of the others renders such practice incomplete.

There are trends within Buddhism today that see the ethical aspects as unimportant once we reach the stage of meditation. It is said that if we start with meditation, the right attitude to the world and to our fellow beings will automatically grow out of this wonderful state. This may be so and it is all right to view things in this way, provided the ethical practices actually happen. If they do not, the meditation is not right and neither is anything else. This is why it is helpful to think of them together as "Right Everything," the everyday practice of Dharma.

The Noble Eightfold Path includes the five basic precepts of the Buddhist life. These are not the "Thou shalt nots" of the Jewish and Christian commandments, but rather an agreement to ". . . undertake the rule of life . . .":

- *not to take or harm life*
- *not to take what is not freely given*
- *not to indulge in sensuality*
- *not to use lying or slanderous speech*
- *not to become intoxicated by using substances that cloud the mind.*

These precepts are now usually undertaken by most Buddhists at the time they "become a Buddhist." The ordained sangha undertake many more.

"Right View" is the knowledge of the Three Signs of Being and the Four Noble Truths. This is the right understanding of the world and our role within it, and from this come the insights that relate to the world we live in. Dharma is concerned with this world we live in today, and not the one in which the Buddha lived over two thousand years ago. Right View is this world of "now," but also the history of the Buddha and all who have achieved the goal that the Buddha taught.

"Right Aim" is our resolve to learn the Dharma, to discover Dharma, to practice Dharma and to share the Dharma with those who wish to discover it. I have a very dear Buddhist friend who would say that, because I am not enlightened, I should not be writing this book. He would probably add that if I were enlightened, then I would not be writing this book. However, for me, writing and sharing the richness that has been given to my life through the Dharma is a part of Right Aim, and something that I have to do.

Right Aim also specifically includes setting our minds on a harmless way of life. What do we mean by a harmless way of life? For me, it includes being a vegetarian. I have been told by some Buddhists that I should not be a vegetarian, as the Buddha ate everything he was given, including meat. This may be true—though I cannot believe it—but Right Aim includes being set on a harmless life, and I find it almost impossible to reconcile the two viewpoints. I am a vegetarian because I believe that it is an expression of compassion, though by no means the whole of it.

The next step, "Right Speech," is the avoidance of lying, slanderous and abusive speech. It is also watching what we say, and as far as possible avoiding "idle babble." I wonder if the Buddha had any knowledge of the level of talk indulged in by polite society. It is certainly hard in the modern world to avoid polite but meaningless social chit-chat without giving offense. However, we need to bear in mind that the precept that evolved from this step was originally aimed at monks who had opted for the homeless life, and there is no criterion by which "idle babble" can be judged in terms of lay life. It is up to each one of us to bear the precept in mind, and to be aware of what we are saying. Then we can still be polite and avoid hurt, while not allowing our tongues to rule our lives.

An adjunct to this step might be to allow ourselves a time of silence at regular intervals. How we do this depends on our circumstances. For example, I like to have music playing while I work, but from time to time I deliberately work in silence, and it is amazing the effect of the contrast. Yet music is also an inspiration for me, and I would not want to avoid it altogether. Everyone will have their own way of finding a time of silence from external noise, though whether we can find silence from our thoughts is another matter.

"Right Action" includes most of the other precepts. Presumably it would also include speech, but the Buddha taught that speech is something that is different enough to have a rule of its own. When we take refuge in the Buddha, the Teaching and the Disciples, we dedicate our body, speech and mind to the journey to enlightenment. Right Action is the equivalent of Right Speech in the realm of the body.

Right Action is the avoidance of taking life or harming, of taking what is not given and of indulgence in sensual misconduct. It also has the positive aspect of the preserving life, caring for those who are sick or suffering, protecting property and respecting the bodies and emotions of others. The Dalai Lama is often reported as saying, "My religion is kindness," and this is also a positive aspect of Right Action.

"Right Livelihood" is an extension of Right Action. It relates to the way in which we earn our living, and care for the worldly needs of ourselves and our families. The Buddha does not specifically include or exclude any professions. He says that Right Livelihood is gained by giving up wrong livelihood. Traditionally, this means avoiding those occupations that involve us in cruelty or the taking of life, in the abuse of Right Speech, in the use of other people for sensual enjoyment or in the selling of drink and drugs. However, here again it is up to us look at what we do for a living, and decide accordingly. In this modern world, it is hard not to contribute in any way to the suffering of others. The Buddhist ideal of Right Livelihood encourages us to keep such suffering and exploitation to a minimum, and avoid it wherever possible.

The term translated as "livelihood" can also mean "pursuits," and this means that the comments above on the suffering of others can also be applied to games, entertainments and other leisure pursuits. Once again we are asked to consider what we are doing, and see whether we can do anything to prevent suffering to those employed to entertain us. Monks are prohibited from music, dancing and other entertainments for this reason, but there is no evidence that the Buddha objected to lay people being entertained or having other enjoyments. The only things we are asked to do is to bear in mind the middle way between excesses of enjoyment and asceticism, and to see whether others suffer in entertaining us.

"Right Effort," the sixth step, is one of the most important steps in Buddhist training.

▶ *In this a disciple of the Buddha will expend his whole energies to generate the willpower to prevent the arising of evil conditions, and to clear those that have already arisen.*

> *Similarly, he does the same to encourage those good conditions that have not yet arisen and to retain and increase those that have already arisen. This . . . is called Right Effort.*

It sounds very simple, but we all know that it is not. In the Christian world, St. Paul summed it up in his letter to the Romans when he said that he does not do the good that he wants to do, but only the evil that he does not want to do. I know this to be true in my own life, and I am sure that most readers will share this experience. Even if he did not have the experience personally, the Buddha was surely aware that will power is not in itself enough to alter our patterns of living. Something else is needed.

In most other religions, there is the concept of "grace" in one form or another. It has often been said that because Buddhism does not recognize a Supreme Power, there is no concept of grace in Buddhism. However grace comes not only from God, but from any enlightened being. It is the positive power or energy that enables us to act in accordance with compassion, and there are many aspects of grace in Buddhism. Channeling of the Buddha's grace is one of the prime functions of the bodhisattva, and one of the principal means whereby living beings are aided towards the release from suffering.

One of the chief channels of grace in Buddhism is that of the Buddha image. The Buddhist author Marco Pallis refers to it as a "reminder of enlightenment."

> ▶ *It is said that several abortive attempts were made to put the Buddha's likeness on record from motives of a personal kind, such as the wish to remember a loved and revered figure and so on . . . . However, in this case the compassion of the Victorious One intervened; he was prepared to allow an image of himself provided this was a true symbol and not a mere reproduction of surfaces—this distinction is very important. Yielding to his devotees' prayers, the Buddha projected his own form miraculously and it was this projection that provided the model for*

a true icon, fit to serve a purpose other than that of personal adulation such as a sacred theme by definition precludes.[2]

Here is a typical case of the action of grace on the lives of devotees. The need is there, even if it is caused by an inadequate understanding of the original teaching, and there is a response that is beyond the normal parameters of experience. Grace is a compassionate response by that which is beyond our conception, which more than makes up for our lack of true understanding. This can also apply to the activities of all Buddhas and Bodhisattvas. The creation of Buddha Lands is also an example of Grace in action within Buddhist teaching. The fact that the Buddha gave us these and similar teachings is proof that he did not see will power as the only way in which we can bring transformation into our lives.

The final two steps on the path, "Right Mindfulness" or "Awareness" and "Right Contemplation" or "Meditation," are dealt with separately. This is not because they are less or more important than the first six, but because with them the emphasis changes. However, it must always be remembered that the Eightfold Path is a whole, and the concept of "Right Everything" needs to be remembered.

The Way Out

Mindfulness

✦

Remember!
How often we forget
To remember.

—SANUKI

*T*he Buddha's teaching of simple mindfulness or awareness as a
way to enlightenment is particularly suitable for people today.
The whole secret of mindfulness can be summed up in the two
words: "Remember!" and "Awareness."

> *Remember to be aware of your breath.*
> *Remember to be aware of where you are.*
> *Remember to be aware of what you are doing.*
> *Remember to be aware of what you say.*
> *Remember to be aware of what you feel.*
> *Remember to be aware of what you think.*

Try it for a little while. Do you see why it is simple to say, but hard
to do?

The key to mindfulness as a form of meditation lies with the
breath. As with many forms of Buddhist meditation, the breath is

used as a vehicle to calm the mind. If you have ever tried to quiet the mind you will be aware of why the Asian traditions refer to the "Monkey Mind." The mind is just like a captive monkey, swinging from branch to branch in its cage, restless, never still. This is particularly so when you try to persuade him to sit still. He is quiet only when he is asleep or when there is some food for him. So, to still the monkey mind we have to give it food, and that food is the breath.

The Buddha's instructions on mindfulness are as follows.

▶ *Mindfully, breathe in, mindfully breathe out.*
Breathing in a long breath, know, "I am breathing in a long breath."
Breathing out a long breath, know, "I am breathing out a long breath."
Breathing in a short breath, know, "I am breathing in a short breath."
Breathing out a short breath, know, "I am breathing out a short breath."
Aware of the whole breath in the body, train yourself to breathe in.
Aware of the whole breath in the body, train yourself to breathe out.
Aware of the calming effect of the whole breath in the body, train
yourself to breathe in.
Aware of the calming effect of the whole breath in the body, train
yourself to breathe out.

Awareness of the breath leads to other avenues of awareness. When you stand, sit, walk or lie down, know what you are doing. When you are eating, drinking, bending or stretching and even going to sleep, know what you are doing. In other words, whatever you are doing be fully aware of it. It should be obvious by now that the Buddha's approach to mindful awareness embraces the whole of life. It is living in the Eternal Present, whatever that may be for each person. All that we need to do is remember.

Any readers who try it will be able to confirm that it is nowhere near as simple as it seems. The moment we try to meditate, to be mindful, is the moment that the monkey seems to become most fractious. Thoughts that we would never have imagined come into our heads. Feelings arise that we did not know we possessed. Memories of events—especially those in which we were hurt in some way—that we have long forgotten are suddenly clearly recalled with the accompanying feelings and emotions. Aches and pains in the body of which we were unaware suddenly become real problems. What do we do with them?

The traditional answer is that if we become aware of them, observe them, but do not react to them, then they will cease to bother us. This is much easier said than done. I know some people find that if they can become aware of these things in a slightly detached and impersonal way, then they fade and eventually disappear. I have found that this can happen, but it does not always do so. If not, then it may be necessary to introduce some other factor such as a change in position, or even practice some other form of meditation. The important thing with regard to mindfulness is that if we choose to make changes we need to be fully aware of what they involve, and of the reasons for our choice.

The Buddha talks of four postures: sitting, standing, walking and lying down. It is important to remember that these four represent the whole of life. Many teachers talk only of sitting meditation, or sometimes of walking meditation. However, the vital essence of mindfulness is that it is a component of every waking moment. Even going to sleep, the bug-bear of most teachings about meditation, is highlighted by the Buddha as an opportunity for mindfulness. It is said that if we can be mindful at the moment sleep overtakes us, our whole time asleep is a meditation.

A similar teaching applies to the moment of dying. In Buddhism death is thought of as being very similar to sleep. If we can die in a state of awareness, then our transition to our next birth, wherever that may be, becomes a conscious one. However, it is not possible to achieve this state of awareness at the last moment, which is why mindfulness is something that we should practice at all times.

▶ *First, sit comfortably—in a chair or on the floor—for a few moments.*
No special posture is required.
In India, sitting cross-legged and upright was normal and natural, but it may not be so for you.
Just be aware of sitting comfortably.

Now become aware of your breathing.
You can be aware of the breath through the rising and falling of the diaphragm,
or by watching the passage of air at the tip of the nose.
Do not try to change it;
mindfulness of breathing is not a breathing exercise.
It may be that as you watch the breath, it will become more gentle, deep and even on its own.
Whichever way you choose, just watch it for a few minutes, without any other aim in view.
If thoughts, emotions, feelings or sounds intrude, note them, and return to watching the breath.
Try not to have any sense of doing it well or badly.
Just do it, and see what happens.

This is the first step in mindfulness. At first do not try it for too long. Five or ten minutes will be fine for a first effort, and even after you have practiced it for some time, do not consciously extend the time. Allow it to grow naturally. Remember that all meditation is a natural state, and nothing should be forced.

▶ *Now stand.*
Let your feet be slightly apart, and be balanced on both of them.
Rock gently from side to side until you feel evenly balanced.
Now become aware of your breathing ... (repeat the steps above).

The only difference with this is that you may not want to do it for longer than three to five minutes at first. Later, as it becomes natural, you may find it a great help when standing in line, or waiting for a bus or train. The only difference with standing awareness practice is that you should do it with your eyes open, and your awareness should extend to the space around you. **Do not do this with eyes closed.**

> ▶ *From the standing position above,*
> *Walk slowly forward some seven to ten paces.*
> *Turn around, being aware of what you are doing,*
> *Of your weight shifting from one foot to the other,*
> *Of the motion of turning.*
> *Pause for a moment, balanced on both feet.*
> *Then set out again, walking slowly back to where you started.*
> *Turn again . . .*
> *Continue walking mindfully like this for five, ten, fifteen or twenty minutes.*

As with the other meditations, it is best to start with a short time and allow it to increase on its own as it feels comfortable.

This meditation is also done with eyes open, with your vision fixed on the ground about six to eight feet in front of you. It is best performed in bare feet, or at least without shoes. If this is not possible for you, you can still do it with shoes on. The important thing is the awareness, and this is made easier if you can feel the floor (or ground) beneath your feet. As you walk slowly be aware of all the feelings that are generated. You may well find that your balance is not as good as you thought it would be. Note this, but do not worry about it. It will improve naturally. Above all, as with any other meditation, if it makes you feel uncomfortable, stop!

The final posture for mindful meditation is lying down. This is often neglected by teachers of meditation, because of the dangers of falling asleep. However, I do not believe that sleep is such a bad thing. If you need sleep, you will probably fall asleep. If it happens on a regular basis, try to note exactly how and when it happens. The goal is awareness of *whatever* happens, and falling asleep is a perfectly natural part of "whatever."

> ▶ *Traditionally, one should lie down on the right side, but this is a matter of individual preference.*
> *Become aware of the action of lying down,*
> *Acknowledge the reasons (for example weariness or pain) that cause you to select this method of meditation.*
> *When you are comfortable, become aware of your breathing as for the sitting meditation, and of your thoughts, emotions and feelings.*
> *If you have practiced sitting meditation, note how this differs from it.*
> *If you feel sleepy, fix the mind more securely on the breath*
> *But don't worry if you do fall asleep.*
> *(In fact, be grateful for it!)*

We have now looked at the four postures of mindfulness, and at the role of the breath as the gateway to awareness. It is said that this practice alone is enough to lead us to enlightenment. However, if the practice appeals to you, it is good to study with a teacher, preferably someone well-versed in the Theravadin tradition, which emphasizes simple mindfulness as a practice, and possibly with a group. Be aware that a teacher might emphasize other aspects of meditation, depending on their experience. In the end, it is your experience that matters most. Remember that meditation is not a cure-all, and the other aspects of the Eightfold Path—or their equivalent in your own faith—should not be forgotten.

Mindfulness has many other applications. A good practice is to be found in the process of eating. I deliberately refer to "the process of eating" rather than just "eating" because this is closer to the idea of what mindfulness is in such a situation. In Zen, it is said: "When you eat, just eat." This is perfectly true. Being mindful is not thinking about an action; it is just being aware of every aspect and letting it impinge upon your mind rather than allowing the mind to impinge upon it.

Reflecting on this, let us consider eating. First of all, most of us tend to eat too quickly. Even when eating is a social occasion devoted to pleasure, it still tends to be secondary to the conversation. In retreat, eating is sometimes done in silence, but this possibility of mindfulness is often spoiled by the imposition of time. For eating to be truly mindful, we need to be unhurried and un-distracted. Then eating becomes the perfect mindfulness exercise, involving all the five senses, or six if you include—as does Buddhism—the mind.

Starting with the sight and smell of the food, sensations arise. The mouth may water (taste), the stomach rumble (hearing), and the mind summon up all kinds of images. As the food is served (touch), there are additional sounds and smells. During the serving, and before actually eating, we can allow thoughts of gratitude to arise, for the people who grow the food, for those who transport it, for those who prepare and cook it, and for the food itself. Eating the food should be a leisurely process. Conveying a portion to the mouth, chewing, tasting, relishing and enjoying are all a part of the process. The spoon or other tools should be at rest during the process, and not busy fishing for the next portion. There are also sounds, smells and the possible requirements of other diners to be aware of, such as the need for passing the salt.

If the meal is not a silent one, then conversation should be limited and relevant. Listening is more important than saying our piece. There may be many other opportunities for mindful eating during the sharing of a meal, but I will not list them, as I am sure I have said more than enough for you to try for yourselves. Further opportunities occur during the clearing and cleaning processes, and it is important not to waste the wonder of a mindful meal with the clamor of chattering afterwards. Instead, allow a space where all that you have discovered during the mealtime can soak into your being and unfold its fruits in your life.

Metta—Loving-Kindness

◆

All the scriptures in thousands of volumes—
they are nothing
but Great Compassion.

—Zuiken

The other major approach to meditation found within the Pali Canon is known as *metta* or the meditation of loving-kindness. This meditation or something similar is also found within all traditions of Buddhism, and even within other faith-traditions. Christ's instructions to "Love our neighbor as ourselves," and all other versions of "The Golden Rule" contain the essence of it. In fact, loving-kindness is in reality the heart of all religion, even if it is frequently not so in practice.

The Buddha clearly told us that this way of meditation is enough to lead us to freedom. "If a monk," he said, "cultivates loving-kindness for as long as the snap of a finger, then he is truly called a disciple of the Buddha." Although this statement refers to monks, I am sure this was because it was addressed to monks, and remembered by monks. Other statements indicate that it refers to anyone, and if this can be said of those who manage it for just a moment, what can be said of those who practice it constantly, and for whom it is the major practice? The Buddha also said that metta includes wisdom meditation, mindfulness and obedience to the teachings of the Buddha.

Shariputra, one of the senior disciples of the Buddha, said that loving-kindness is the way of escape from all ill-will, and it would be reasonable to assume that he had heard this teaching from the Buddha himself.

▶ *When you have the freedom of loving-kindness in your heart, it is impossible for ill-will to invade and remain. When loving-kindness is maintained in the heart, when it is fostered, cultivated, and used as one's vehicle [for meditation] ill-will will find no place in the heart, for the heart-freedom of loving-kindness is the escape from all ill-will.*

What is this metta or loving-kindness? It is the intention to wish all beings well, and the feeling that comes from it. It includes yourself, those you love, others that you know, and in particular those who might have harmed or upset you. Note that it includes the feeling that comes from the intention. When I have been teaching metta meditation, people have said to me that they feel that it is in some way hypocritical or dishonest, as they cannot feel goodwill towards some people. This is perfectly normal. Unless we are in some way enlightened, we can only start by making the intention with our thoughts and words to generate and share this goodwill towards those we do not like or understand.

We have to start from where we are. Jesus told us to "Love our neighbors *as ourselves*" (my italics). Yet how often have we been told, particularly in our early lives, that it is wrong to love ourselves. Even though the Buddha told us that we do not have "selves," he was clear that while we live with the illusion of self and others, then we must develop love for "all beings," and this must include ourselves. Modern psychology has discovered that we cannot love others if we do not love ourselves, confirming the teaching of the Buddha and Jesus as well as of other enlightened teachers through the ages.

This does not mean being selfish. It means the very reverse. One of the principal ways to lose pre-occupation with our selves is to selflessly serve others, so that eventually both self and other are replaced by a universal and unconditional compassion in which loving-kindness naturally flows without thought. Loving our neighbors must also include consideration for what they would want, and not what we think is good for them.

There are many approaches to metta meditation, and it depends on your belief which way you choose. If you have a belief in God, then you can adapt the traditional Buddhist method to invoke Divine Love to aid your own efforts. Remember, however, that our intention starts the whole thing off. (If God is Love, then God is already all the loving that can be.)

If you wish to use the traditional Buddhist method, then it is best to start by reflecting on the words of the Buddha in the *Metta Sutra*.

▶ *In safety and bliss*
may all beings be happy.
Whatever beings there may be
Be they weak or strong,
Excepting none,
Short, tall or middle-sized,
Large or small,
Seen or unseen,
Dwelling far or near,
Born or yet to be born;
May they all be happy.

It cannot be said too many times that "all beings" includes yourself, your friends, your enemies, animals, insects, all living beings; male, female or of an indeterminate sex, incarnate, discarnate or beings from the angelic or diabolical realms that have never been on earth. The greatest historical villains need to be included. It has been said by a Christian mystic that the greatest problem the Church has ever had is that it has never forgiven Judas, so if you are a Christian, you might start there. Your next-door neighbor who lets his hedge grow too high, or their rooster who crows at four o'clock in the morning when you want to sleep in are also included. If you hate spiders, snakes or any other creature, make an effort to include them. "All Beings" means *all* beings.

The Buddha also gave instructions that we should consciously extend our loving-kindness to the six directions, North, South, East, West, Above and Below. Once we have generated loving-kindness, we should send it to each of the quarters in turn, and literally flood them with our goodwill and compassion.

It may be asked what good all this will do. Is it only a practice that benefits myself, or do other beings gain benefit from it? Maybe this is not a question that should be asked—just do it, is the advice my teacher gave—but it is one that is normal for Westerners, brought up with the concept of prayer (whether you believe in it or not). I personally believe that the world is a better place when people practice metta meditation. Even if it only benefits ourselves it is worth doing, as is any practice that leads to enlightenment.

> ❯ *Start by thinking of yourself, your body and mind.*
> *Think of yourself as someone that you love.*
> *Wish yourself well in every way.*
> *Flood your body—particularly any areas that are suffering—with thoughts of love and compassion.*
> *As you breathe in, fill your mind with thoughts of peace,*
> *and as you breathe out, think of letting go of stress and tension.*
> *"May I be well and happy, and may my mind be at peace."*
> *Dwell on these thoughts for a few minutes.*

Now think of someone you love.
Think of them, and send them your love and compassion, wishing them
well.
"May they be well and happy, and may their minds be at peace."
Dwell on these thoughts for a few minutes.

Now think of someone you know, but do not know well.
Think of them, and send them your love and compassion, wishing them
well.
"May they be well and happy, and may their minds be at peace."
Dwell on these thoughts for a few minutes.

Now think of someone you hate or resent.
Think of them, and send them your love and compassion, wishing them
well.
Even if you cannot feel this, make the intention in your mind.
"May they be well and happy, and may their minds be at peace."
Dwell on these thoughts for a few minutes.

Now think of the world to the East, and of all beings who dwell there.
Think of them, and send them your love and compassion, wishing them
well.
"May they be well and happy, and may their minds be at peace."
Dwell on these thoughts for a few minutes.

Now think of the world to the West, and of all beings who dwell there.
Think of them, and send them your love and compassion, wishing them
well.
"May they be well and happy, and may their minds be at peace."
Dwell on these thoughts for a few minutes.

Now think of the world to the North, and of all beings who dwell there.
Think of them, and send them your love and compassion, wishing them
well.
"May they be well and happy, and may their minds be at peace."
Dwell on these thoughts for a few minutes.

Now think of the world to the South, and of all beings who dwell there.
Think of them, and send them your love and compassion, wishing them
well.
"May they be well and happy, and may their minds be at peace."
Dwell on these thoughts for a few minutes.

Now think of the world above you, and of all beings who dwell there.
Think of them, and send them your love and compassion, wishing them
well.
"May they be well and happy, and may their minds be at peace."
Dwell on these thoughts for a few minutes.

Now think of the world below you, and of all beings who dwell there.
Think of them, and send them your love and compassion, wishing them
well.
"May they be well and happy, and may their minds be at peace."
Dwell on these thoughts for a few minutes.

Close by saying or thinking;
"May all beings be well and happy.
May they know joy, and peace, love and compassion.
May any merit gained from this practice be shared with them,
and may they attain their Supreme Goal."

And finally, remember with gratitude,
"I am one of those beings."

Meditation—East and West

✦

Zen and Shin
Two sides
Of the same coin.

—JACK AUSTIN

There are millions of Buddhists in the world who would say that they do not meditate. However, it all depends on what we mean by "meditation." For example, is someone meditating who comes into a temple and offers incense with a focused mind, or who sits and gazes at the image of the Buddha with great love and devotion, or who single-mindedly chants the name of the Buddha? In reality, meditation applies to the whole of life, and any religious or even artistic practice that is carried on with a focused mind.

It is a common fallacy that there is no tradition of meditation in the West, and therefore the role of Buddhism is to teach meditation to Christians and others. Buddhism has added a richness to the variety of meditation that has always been available in Western traditions, although not widely known. One thing the arrival of Buddhism has done is to re-awaken interest in Western methods of meditation. However, the teaching is not only one way; Buddhists can also learn from European traditions.

There are differences in Eastern and Western approaches to meditation, and in the language used. The Western tradition involves using the mind to think about or ponder a subject. Meditation often leads to contemplation, in which the still mind dwells on an object or on the formless nature of things. Some Western writers describe this process as "contemplative meditation." This peculiarly Western way of meditation is not well-known within Buddhism, but since I learned in a Christian retreat, I have discovered many references to something similar in Buddhist practice. Because it is one of my favorite ways of meditation, I would like to share it with you.

This technique is helpful in that it stimulates the intuition (intuition means "inner teaching") and much of the Buddha's teaching can only be understood in this way. Although I learned this way of meditation from a Christian source, the practice of "deep listening" is in fact also a Buddhist one. Take a word or phrase and allow the mind to think about it. Call to mind all the meanings that you know, all the contexts in which it applies and any other thoughts that relate to it. Do not be afraid to include "I don't know"; honesty is most important. If the mind wanders, bring it gently back to the subject. As we allow the mind to do its work it gradually ceases to wander, and there is a certain delight in the process.

> ▶ *Form is emptiness, emptiness is form.*
> *This is what the Buddha said.*
> *We now know that this is scientifically true*
> *That what appears as matter is in fact energy.*
> *This energy is the universal truth about all form.*
> *We are also taught that all things have Buddha Nature.*
> *Buddha Nature is unborn, unmade, unmanifest and unbecome,*
> *It is the way out of the born, made manifest and become.*
> *Form is emptiness, emptiness is form.*
> *Form is energy, energy is form.*
> *This body is form, it is matter,*
> *But in Reality it is emptiness*

As is everything else I think about myself.
Form is a part of the reality
But it is not the Reality.
What is?

After a while the mind will exhaust all that it knows, and will become still. At this stage, a listening attitude will develop. This attitude is in fact the mind saying, "There! I've done all I can do. I don't know anything else." Into this inner silence can come a variety of experiences, from a "still small voice" speaking words that shed new light on the subject to a sense of release like a deep sigh. If our intuition— in Buddhist terms the Unborn Buddha Mind—speaks, the words may be familiar, but they will still be new.

Another approach to meditation that is practiced in both Eastern and Western traditions is that of visualization. There are many Buddhist practices of visualization, the best-known of which are in the Tibetan traditions. These vary from simply imagining the form of a Buddha or Bodhisattva to complex tantric practices whereby the form eventually merges with the meditator. The former is quite harmless and can be very helpful, but the latter can be dangerous without proper instruction. I can confirm this, having known people who have tried to do these visualizations using instructions from books only to find themselves in severe states of stress and even illness. I cannot recommend any of these books as I am clear that tantric visualization should be learned only from a teacher who has followed this path through to its goal, and is authorized to teach it.

This does not mean that all visualization is dangerous. What I am warning against is the imposition of unknown powers into the being of a meditator who is not prepared to cope with them. Most of us will not dabble with electricity or gas without the proper knowledge and safety precautions. With some of these tantric practices we are dealing with energies that are potentially as dangerous, or even more so because they affect the mind as well as the body. Properly qualified teachers are able to discern what a student can cope with, and will encourage the student to meditate only on those qualities. They will also give all the preparatory purification exercises and ensure that they are done properly. Impatience is a common human failing, and left to our own devices we have no way to ensure that we are doing all aspects of the practice correctly.

Safe visualization practices that allow us to contemplate the forms of Buddhas and Bodhisattvas external to ourselves, and even to receive blessings from them, can be most helpful. If there is a form of a Buddha or Bodhisattva that intuitively appeals to us it is fine to contemplate a picture or image, and then to visualize them. This kind of visualization is practiced in most of the world religions that allow forms of saints or deities, and followers can testify to the many blessings that are achieved by such practices. In the example that follows I will speak of the Buddha, but you can substitute any Buddha, Bodhisattva or other great being in the Buddhist or other traditions.

▶ *Relax, and sit comfortably.*
Watch your breathing for a while,
Breathing in with awareness, and out with relaxation.

Imagine a form of the Buddha before you.
One you can easily call to mind.
He sits or stands before you, radiating peace and serenity.
You pay reverence to him in whatever way you feel is respectful,
Maybe you bow, or offer incense, flowers or fruit.
Your respect is acknowledged by a compassionate smile.
The Buddha is full of compassion,
With a spiritual friendliness that overcomes any fear that you may have.
You know you could ask questions, as did the disciples of old,
Or you can allow him to know your unspoken thoughts.
If you do either of these, then listen deep within yourself for the answer.

*You can also just sit or stand in silence, soaking up the peace of his
presence.
Rays of light are emitted from his head to your head,
From his throat to your throat,
From his heart to your heart,
Purifying body speech and mind.*

*Hold this vision as long as is comfortable.
Relax and do not strain.
When you feel it is right,
Allow the visualization to fade into a rainbow of color
That blesses you.*

*Slowly return to your everyday consciousness.
Stretch and give thanks,
Sharing your blessings with all suffering beings.*

As you finish this or any other meditation it is a good idea to allow
your eyes to open slowly, and then to look around. When teaching
people how to end their meditation I usually encourage them to
clench their fists, stretch out the fingers, then the arms and have a
good stretch with the whole body. Finally, we join the palms prayer-
wise, give thanks for blessings received, and make the intention to
share them with all other suffering beings.

Sharing the blessings is an essential part of all forms of Buddhist
meditation. We do not meditate for ourselves alone. This intention
to share the fruits of meditation is called "merit," and it is something
we share on all possible occasions. If meditation develops insight
and wisdom, the sharing of merit develops compassion. It is the
Buddha's teaching that both are essential for enlightenment.

Zen

✦

Without practicing
Practice Suchness;
This is the true practice.

—Zuiken

Z en is often presented as being something Asian and mysterious.
It is not. Zen is simply the word "meditation." In Sanskrit, the
word is *dhyana*, the final "a" being silent. Buddhism went from India
to China, where dhyana was pronounced phonetically as *"Ch'an."*
When this was written down pictographically and taken to Japan, it
was pronounced "Zen."

I am tempted to say that this is all there is to it, but no one
would believe me. Yet this is what my teachers have told me. However, my experience tells me that Zen is a lot more and even a lot less.
Zen is everything or nothing; and everything and nothing. However
mysteriously or esoterically it is presented, Zen is essentially very
ordinary. It is the essence of ordinariness. Yet it is the most extraordinary thing in the world. There are problems in saying what Zen is
in words, because originally its main point was that it was transmitted
"without words."

The story goes that towards the end of his life the Buddha stood before his disciples, and idly twirled a flower in his fingers. Perhaps he should have known better. None of those present saw anything significant in his actions except Mahakasyapa, who smiled (though one version says that he tried not to). Mumon, in his *Gateless Gate*[3], a commentary on various Zen stories, says caustically that certainly he should have known better. Anyway, the Buddha did not stay silent but gave a speech in which he proclaimed that the true teaching was beyond words, and that he had given it to Mahakasyapa. My teacher Sanuki said that both of them should have known better.

From all this nonsense came the whole lineage of Ch'an and Zen patriarchs from which today's teachers claim succession. Zen is by nature iconoclastic, and the Zen Master Mumon says of this wonderful event

▶ *This Buddha thought he could cheat everyone.*
He sold dog-meat as best lamb.
What if the whole gathering had laughed together?
Would the essence have been transmitted to them all?
And if Mahakasyapa had not smiled, would the teaching have been transmitted at all?
If Buddha says the teaching can be transmitted, he is a con-artist, and if he says it cannot, why did he approve Mahakasyapa's smile?

When it comes to Zen there is really nothing new to say, so all I can do is to share the wisdom and insight that has been given by those who have guided me on this razor-edged path. They are all people I respect, not so much because of what they have said, but because of what they are. Emerson is reported to have said, "What you are speaks so loud, I cannot hear what you say." The same thing occurs in the story of the student who went to study with a Hasidic Rabbi, and said that he did not go to hear his teaching but to see the way he tied his shoelaces. What my teachers have said is important, but it is a finger pointing to the moon. Sometimes their words gave me a great peace and stillness, and sometimes they made me laugh out loud. They may do the same for you.

Let us start by looking at one or two definitions of Zen, and hoping that they will mean something. I doubt if they will by themselves, but sometimes such paradoxical words have a meaning that goes beyond the mind into what modern psychologists call "lateral thinking," or pure insight without reasoning. There have been Zen masters who achieved their insight by hearing a passage from the sutras, or a poem, or by the answer to a koan or nonsense riddle, often used in Zen to bring revelation. There have been those who have been enlightened by the sound of water, the sight of the moon, a blow, a joke, or just by seeing the ridiculous nature of life. If life is dukkha, then dukkha certainly has its funny side, or most comedians would be out of a job. Life is also changing, and then it is the unexpected that often makes us laugh.

In his wonderful book, *Zen Flesh, Zen Bones*, the first book I ever read on Zen and the one that convinced me that this was something I needed, Paul Reps leaves the question, "What is Zen?" until the last page. Then his answer is to tell us that Zen cannot be defined, but is something that is universal and comes of itself.

> ▶ *Instantly mind frees. How it frees! . . . Look at it this way, inside out and outside in: CONSCIOUSNESS everywhere, inclusive, through you. Then you can't help living humbly, in wonder.*

This idea of universal consciousness is the key. It is why many Zen masters will not allow that Zen is anything but ordinary life. "When I am hungry I eat; when thirsty I drink; when tired I lay down and sleep." "Doesn't everyone?" I hear you reply. Yes, they do, but how many other things are they doing or thinking at the same time, and how much of a sense of wonder do they have for actions that are ordinary and mundane?

Sanuki used to teach us *zazen* or seated meditation in a bare room with a single scroll hanging in the corner. In front was a small table on which were some flowers and a stick of incense. The scroll contained a single Japanese character, painted in black ink in a flowing style. When newcomers asked what it meant, they were told that it contained the essence of his teaching. "Yes, but what does it mean?" they would ask. Then he would look fierce, and growl, "Remember!" before dissolving into infectious laughter in which everyone—including the newcomer—would join.

Most Zen groups today are concerned with providing conditions for zazen. This is mostly performed in the Japanese style on the floor, sitting erect in either the cross-legged lotus position, or kneeling, with great attention paid to posture. Between sitting meditation there are times of walking meditation, either slowly or quickly depending on the tradition. On retreat there are strict rules about working, sleeping and eating. Some traditions work on the practice of "just sitting" holding that the practice itself is the awareness of our Buddha Nature. Others work on koans, which are either stories of the old Zen masters or nonsense riddles designed to tease the mind into a state of stillness in which the meditator can recognize what has been there all the time.

Sanuki did teach us sitting meditation, though he was happy for us to use chairs. He would also take us to a Christian church to meditate, or for walks in the park. He would teach the Zen of floor-sweeping, of cooking, eating and washing-up, of the tea—and coffee—ceremony. None of this was done in a formal way, and there was much spontaneity and laughter in his teaching. He would not say much about himself, not even his real name (Sanuki was a nickname based on the district that he came from). He did reluctantly tell us that he had left the temple, where he still had friends, because he could no longer take the formality and ritual that he felt were stifling the true spirit of Zen. For him, Zen was life, and could not be contained within a temple or the formal rules of religion, though he recognized that some people needed such discipline. I knew him only for a short time before he went back to Japan for his father's funeral, and was himself killed in a car crash.

The great thing about his teaching was always to remember. Remember our Buddha Nature, remember the Unborn Buddha Mind, remember the Great Compassion and remember the Presence of God within us. Yes, he did speak of God. For him, God was everything, and he knew that most of us had come from Christian backgrounds where we put limitations on God. Sanuki was not a careful user of words, and would not worry about contradicting himself if it helped an individual to understand. His teaching was essentially beyond words. If you have a feeling that your spiritual life is too serious, that there is something missing, or that there are too many words, then it may be that the Zen Way is for you.

However, be warned. If you go to a Zen center, it may be that you will find the same and more. If you feel at home with the traditional Asian formality and discipline, it may be that this is what you need. If you find it restricting and humorless, and lacking the freedom that you seek, do not worry. There are other ways. As you are reading this, you might like to begin your search—as many of us have done—with a few of the books mentioned in the bibliography. Then you will either say with relief, "This is for me," or you will know there is another path that you should be seeking. Later chapters may help. If it is true that Zen cannot be found in books, then neither can it be found in temples, Buddha images, robes, ceremonies or zazen. All are fingers pointing to the moon; fine if you don't confuse the finger and the moon.

Zen is your life, here and now, where you are. It is only a question of changing your view. Within this world of dukkha is a world where Mara, the traditional devil of Buddhist thought, is sent packing by laughter. If anything is too holy to laugh at, it is too holy.

Occasionally Mara is persuaded to share the great joke. And the great joke is this; you already are that which you are seeking. The special thing you are seeking is really nothing special. And the ordinary is the most extraordinary thing in the world.

Reflect on this!

▶ *The Buddha told this story:*

There once was a traveler who was chased by a tiger.
He was a good runner, but the tiger was swifter, and gained on him.
Suddenly they came to a sheer cliff.
The traveler caught hold of a vine growing on the edge, and, just in time, swung himself over the edge and out of the tiger's reach.
The tiger paced back and forth growling, but could not reach him.
Just as the traveler was congratulating himself, he heard another growl.
Below him, was another tiger.
A little mouse came out of a hole in the cliff, and began to gnaw at the vine. The traveler watched in horror as it began to eat through it.
He looked around, and saw that growing beside him were some luscious wild strawberries.
He reached out, picked one and ate it.
How delicious!

The Koans of Life

◆

To prune roses is good,
To prune a priest is better.
Cut off his head
And his heart will speak.

—TOKUZAN

Occasionally a book has come into my life that is not widely recognized as a masterpiece of the spiritual life, but that has had an impact on me that is almost beyond words. Such a book was *The Goose Is Out* by W. J. Gabb. First published in 1956, it was reissued in paperback in 1972 but now, sadly, is out of print. I first came across a copy soon after it was published and I have lived with it ever since.

Though I never met him, Bill Gabb was a teacher to me in every sense of the word. He taught me more through this little book than I can ever say. His theme was that Zen is a way of providing answers to the problems of everyday life, that can be viewed in the same way as the koans or nonsense riddles that are the subjects of meditation in Zen Buddhism. The Zen practitioner struggles with the koans until a breakthrough is achieved. The same approach can be used with the problems of everyday life, and the breakthrough is a form of special magic that is at the same time very ordinary.

I said that I have lived with this book, and it is true. I have practiced—when I remember—the suggestions that the author gives, and have found that they work. I have personally discovered their magic, and found that they help me to discover the extraordinary heart in ordinary things. I have been fortunate in my teachers, all of whom have emphasized in different ways the ability of the Buddha's teaching to enrich everyday life, but none have pointed out more clearly that everyday life is the teacher.

The first part of the book is autobiographical, and tells the story of the author's spiritual quest for the meaning of suffering through teachings of positive thinking and spiritual healing, and ending with his discovery of Zen Buddhism. His is not a Zen that takes us away from the world, yet he does see his practice within a monastery.

▶ *I will say how it is with me.*

I move and have my being in a Zen monastery which I call the world. Around me are all the other monks, the human inhabitants of this planet, many of whom are still ignorant but some of whom I recognize as enlightened in their degree.

In this monastery I am subject to privations, austerities and hard work, with little leisure and long vigils. I move amid beauty and horror.

. . . Daily I meet the Master who presides over this community of mankind and hourly I ponder the problems he has set me to solve. Some of them are koans which are not capable of logical solution, but all admit of an answer, Sometimes, all too frequently, the Master slaps my face. Occasionally I return the blow. And sometimes, when I least expect it, he brings me tea and cake.

Who is this Master? When I was in the womb he overshadowed me, and ever since I left it I have turned to him instinctively as a babe turns to the mother, not knowing the nature of the relationship but clinging to the breast. Most of my fellow-men are still in the instinctive stage, clinging with their eyes shut like new-born kittens, but a number have recognized the relationship even though their concepts are not very clear. As for me, I know him quite simply as my life.

This passage had an incredible impact on me. It confirmed my approach to the Dharma. I do not have to go to Japan, India or Tibet, go into a monastery, wear robes, or give a large part of my day to formal meditation in order to live the Zen—and thus the Buddhist—life. It tells me that I do not have to entrust myself to another human being for my spiritual journey, just because I have been led to believe they are enlightened. It tells me that right here and now, where I am, is what I need, *provided I view it in the right way.*

In relation to this, Gabb tells the story of a dream. He dreamt that he was being charged by a huge bull elephant. Instead of being afraid, he waved his pocket handkerchief at it, it shrank in size and they had a friendly conversation. On waking, he decided to deal with real-life troubles in the same way. He had great success in waving a symbolic pocket handkerchief at them, at which they proved to be made only of mind-stuff, and easily dissolved back to where they had come from.

I have tried this and it works. I do not use the pocket handkerchief, but I try to remember to smile and bear in mind that things are usually not as bad as they look. This works only if I remember to do it right at the beginning, before I have had a chance to feel fear or anger. It seems that fear and anger set the reality of the situation in the mind, so it is important to respond before this can happen. I discovered that if I practice this technique on small things, so that when faced with big ones it becomes easier to remember. It is also linked with intuition, that "still small voice" that seems to know things that our minds cannot, and that provides guidance for living.

For example, when I lived in London there was a ten-minute walk down a straight road from my home to the bus stop. Sometimes I would see a bus draw up when I was still a few minutes away. Being late, and knowing that it usually waited there for a short while, I would run and catch the bus. Sometimes an inner voice would say, "don't run; it's all right." I would ignore it and run for the bus, which would sit there even longer than usual, while two or three other buses would go past. This happened so many times that at last I learned the lesson, and I got quite good at intuitively judging the right bus to catch for the quickest journey.

This sort of thing is all right for the small questions, and even for the bigger ones of daily life. But what about the very big questions, such as the Buddha's, "Why is there suffering?" or "Is there a way out of suffering?" At the root of these questions lies the original Great Koan, "Who or what am I?" This is always with us. While we may not find the ultimate answer as the Buddha did, we can find answers that will help our lives to be more harmonious. We have to remember that the answers given by our intuition are provisional, and relate to here and now. They may not be the same tomorrow or next week.

Some of my Buddhist friends say that such here and now answers are no answers at all, but I do not agree. Answers are answers, and anything that helps—even in a small way—to relieve suffering is for me in the spirit of the Dharma. I go back to the basic guidance of the Kalama Sutra, and seek answers that are good and helpful here and now.

Gabb also tells the story of how he was asked from time to time to "say a word" for friends of his who were in trouble. The only question he asked himself was, "Is it right for me to do this?"—and only if he received the inspiration did he do so. Even then, "the word" varied. Once it was "Mu," a negative term that is one of the great Zen koans, while another time he felt it right to go into a church and pray as he had done when a child. There was no reason for all this, it was just the right thing to do at the time, and achieved the required result.

The second part of The Goose Is Out contains the "Tales of Tokuzan." These stories came to the author in moments of inspired reverie. He thought he had invented the name Tokuzan from the names of two Chinese Buddhist sages, and only later found that there really was such a person. Like all Zen tales they are teaching stories, but they teach by paradox rather than logic, taking the mind beyond the realm of reason.

One of my favorites, which continues the theme of Zen in the world, is called "The Hermit."

> ▶ *Tokuzan was walking through the market of a nearby town. He noticed in particular a vendor of millet-seed vociferously shouting the virtues of his commodity. Finally, he entered into conversation with the man, and was surprised by his wise remarks.*
>
> *"For a vendor of millet-seed you make an admirable philosopher," he observed.*
>
> *"As a hermit, I have plenty of time for meditation," the man agreed.*
>
> *"Did you say 'hermit'?" asked the Master, thinking he had misheard. The man waved his hand to the jostling crowd and recited:*
>
> > *"Owing to the exigencies of circumstance,*
> > *The last remnants of my privacy have been removed.*
> > *Now*
> > *My seclusion is complete."*
>
> *"Remarkable," said Tokuzan. "Will you please explain?"*
>
> *The man continued, "Long time since, I wished to retire from the world and become a hermit. However, I was smitten with love-sickness, and took a wife instead. She bore me many children, including several fine but noisy sons. Still I longed for seclusion in which to meditate, but the demands that my family necessarily made upon me increased, and my leisure hours became less and less. Finally, when all my time was occupied, I went away, and now I live in the bosom of my family and the clamor of the market. I doubt if I shall come back." He proffered a handful of millet-seeds.*
>
> *Tokuzan marvelled as he accepted the seeds. "In the whole of China I would say you have no equal."*
>
> *Good-humoredly, the man remonstrated, "In the whole of China there is none else but I."*

Such teaching helps me to be "in the world but not of it." There is a tendency in some Buddhist circles to think of monks and nuns as the only ones who dedicate their lives to the search for enlightenment. This story points to the possibility of being a contemplative while fulfilling our karma in the world. Finding peace of mind is not easy, whether in a monastery or in the midst of a busy life. Yet the monastic life can also be of practical help in a suffering world, as this next story, "A Zen Word," illustrates.

▶ *Famine was in the land. Vegetables were scarce and rice all but unobtainable. Tokuzan, himself weakened through privation, wandered through the villages, giving comfort where he could, but always sick at heart. Eventually there met him one Chan, formerly a lay monk, who knew the Master by repute. Chan asked him to enter his house, and there on a mat lay his little son, a child too weak to walk. The man pointed to the protruding bones and bloated belly, and his question was not one to which he expected an answer: "Is there a Zen word to fit this circumstance?"*

"There is a Zen Word to fit every circumstance," said the Master. "Bring an ox-cart and take him to the monastery. I eat little and can do with less. He shall sit at my table, and share my bowl. In time he will be strong."

Chan made obeisance to the ground. "I see the word in works."

Later, as they traveled with the lad, Chan ventured: "Master, is there also a Zen word for the need for the word in works? Can Zen say why this thing must be, why must we suffer so?"

Tokuzan said, "There is a substance for every symbol, and a word for every need. But a man may not see this word in works, he must hear it said in truth."

"In time shall I hear it said?" asked the man. He thought of long and fruitless hours spent in meditation, and his question was a sigh.

A breeze swept the long grass by the roadside. The sound echoed the sigh as the grass whispered the eternal secret. Tokuzan told him, "You will, but not in 'time.'"

Reading this, I too think of long and fruitless hours spent in meditation, and of all the effort that I have put into seeking the Buddha's "word." I think of others who have admitted that they have similarly sought the secret in vain. From this I realize that there is always something else, something that provides what is missing. I confess my ignorance, admitting that the answer to all these great questions is "I don't know." In that emptying I see that I too have been seeking it "in time," although it is only in the timeless that I can ever find it. If I cannot do it alone, maybe the Buddha has the power that can help me.

Another Way—
Pure Land Buddhism
◆

To live
Is to recite the Nembutsu.
No other practice is necessary.

—TAIRYU FURUKAWA

At some stage in my Buddhist life, I realized that I was not getting anywhere. I was not even sure if there was anywhere to get to. I had practiced meditation in a number of different traditions and, while this did help me somewhat, there was still a feeling of dissatisfaction. Maybe this was as it should be. After all, was this not the essence of dukkha? I spoke to Buddhist and non-Buddhist friends and some confirmed that they had similar feelings, while others did not know what I was talking about.

This is not an unusual state of affairs. I have met many people on the Buddhist path who have had similar experiences. What is different is what people do about it. Some may explore another tradition, or find another teacher; or perhaps discover that Buddhism is not for them. All these responses are fine. It does not matter to me whether or not people call themselves Buddhists. I am concerned only that they find their way out of suffering.

I was lucky enough to discover a way of Buddhist thought and practice that emphasized the power of the Buddha's enlightenment to help us. Jesus pointed his followers towards God, and spoke of God as Unconditional Love. The Buddha's Power is that of Universal Compassion, but Love and Compassion are really One. Through this compassion, many Buddhists believe that their next birth can be in one of a number of Buddha-lands: places where their progress to enlightenment is assured, and where there are none of the distractions that beset us in this world.

Amitabha, the Buddha of Infinite Light, otherwise known as *Amitayus*, Infinite Life (*Amida* in Japanese) has possibly the greatest following among Buddhists in China, Japan and Tibet. His story is told in three sutras revealed by Shakyamuni: *The Larger* and *Smaller Sukhavativyuha Sutras* and the *Contemplation Sutra*. Amida's Light shines unimpeded throughout all the universe, while his Life is always present and undying. In fact, Amida is more than just a being. He (though really it is incorrect to say "He," we have to start somewhere) is Infinite Light and Eternal Life itself. Amida also has many other titles such as Boundless Light, Unhindered Light, Light of Joy and Light of Wisdom. The concept of Light is very important in this tradition, but it is not the visible light that we know as the opposite of darkness.[4]

Pure Land Buddhism is not separate from mainstream Buddhism. In the Mahayana tradition when a Buddha becomes enlightened, he acquires a Dharma-Body without losing his human body. According to the Larger Sutra, before he became enlightened, Amitabha was a bodhisattva called *Dharmakara* (Dharma Treasury). He vowed that when he became a Buddha he would create a Buddha-land called *Sukhavati*—the Pure or Happy Land, where all who are born there are certain to become Buddhas. Amida Buddha gained a Dharma-Body when he became a Buddha, and this Dharma-Body became Sukhavati. Instead of incarnating on the Earth, Amida chose to continue to serve suffering beings in his own land.

Because the Pure Land is the Dharma-Body of Amida, it has two aspects. It is a place in which we can be reborn after our present life is over, and also as a state of being in the here and now. Birth in the Pure Land is the result of the power of Amida's vow, and we can accept it at any time. It is not necessary for us to die before we can personally experience that power. The combination of these two aspects is one of the principal appeals of this tradition.

I cannot prove any of this to be true. Having come to Buddhism because it did not demand anything of me in the way of faith, how could I have been attracted by an approach that would require me to believe many things that were historically impossible? The answer is that this story is a mythological approach to an eternal truth; the truth that the Light of Wisdom is infinite, and the Life of Compassion is eternal. Myths can penetrate deeper than facts, and the story cuts through the reasoning mind. For me, it is experience that is important. My experience is that this Light is a significant factor in my life. Not as a blinding flash, but as a compassionate presence that helps in my daily activities. It is a glimpse of Buddha-Nature.

The Sutras tell us that we can be born in the Pure Land by meditating on Amida's form and reciting his name. The main practice today in the Pure Land traditions in China and Japan is that of *Nembutsu*, or saying the Name. The way I was taught it was *Namo Amida Buddha*. Namo literally means "I take refuge in the Holy Name." Chanting the Name is often incorporated into a *puja* or service, where offerings are made. These are usually candle, incense and flowers, symbolizing the Light of the Buddha, the Fragrance of the Dharma and Beauty of the Sangha. Extracts from one of the sutras are chanted, and merit is dedicated to the welfare of all suffering beings. The Name may be chanted for an extended time. Such services take place in temples but also, more importantly, daily in the homes of millions of Buddhists today.

Pure Land Buddhism presents a philosophy and practice that is very different from most other approaches to Buddhism. In the Japanese *Jodoshinshu* (True Pure Land) or *Shin* school, the largest, it is primarily a non-monastic tradition. Its teachings particularly apply to lay men and women who live and work in the everyday world. There are priests who serve temples, but both priests and lay-people are seen as disciples of the Buddha.

Most Westerners who come to Pure Land Buddhism do so because our previous Buddhist study and practice have not fulfilled our hopes. We are not enlightened, and do not feel that we are even on the way. Our compassion is at best partial, and all this is because, according to Pure Land Buddhism, we have relied on our own efforts. The Pure Land Tradition asks us to honestly face our shortcomings in the field of spiritual progress, and recognize our inadequacy in progressing towards enlightenment. Once we have done this, we can surrender all of ourselves to the compassionate power of the Buddha. We can only surrender what we know. Until we look at who we are and where we are we do not know what to surrender. This surrender is actually a most important part of Buddhist practice.

Acceptance of this approach was not immediate for me. However, it gradually began to become more and more real as I met with other Buddhists who were following this path, and began the remembrance of the Buddha and development of gratitude as a daily practice. Following this path has led me to meet some of the most enlightened yet humble people, who have about them the atmosphere of serenity that I would like to develop.

Pure Land Buddhism is many-sided. Chinese schools link chanting of the Buddha's name with other practices, such as visualization or Ch'an (Zen) meditation. They see it as a vehicle to still the mind, and allow Buddha's Light within to be revealed. Japanese schools tend towards the surrendering of all other practices. Humility born of self-knowledge is all important. Honen, the founder of the *Jodoshu* (Pure Land School) was very clear.

▶ *You may have carefully studied all the teachings that Shakyamuni taught during his lifetime, but if you entrust yourself to the Nembutsu, then you should—by turning yourself into a foolish person who does not know even a single written character—simply say the Nembutsu with wholeness of heart, free from any pretensions to wisdom.*

Shinran, the founder of the Jodoshinshu, emphasized the mystical aspect that particularly appeals to me. Amida made his vows that he would save all beings when he attained Buddhahood. Amida is a Buddha, so we are *already* saved, and there is no need for us to "do" anything to bring about our birth in the Pure Land. Instead, we need to "undo"; to let go of all our self-power and efforts to become enlightened, as they get us nowhere. As we let go of our own efforts, we are grasped by the Light of Amida's Compassion, and our birth in the Pure Land is assured. This state is called *Shinjin*.

Honen and Shinran caused a stir among the powerful monastic authorities. They were exiled, and wandered among the ordinary uneducated people such as farmers and fishermen, who were at that time actually barred from becoming Buddhists. This was partly because they could not read the scriptures and partly because of their occupations, which involved killing. It must have been amazing for them to be visited by these learned monks, to hear about the compassion of the Buddha, and to learn that they too could embrace Buddhism simply by reciting the name of the Buddha. When Honen and Shinran came back to the capital, they both wrote learned works to justify their teaching to scholars, but I feel it is the simple teaching that is their true legacy.

▶ *A monk saw an old woman walking past him on her way to her Pure Land temple.*

He called out:
"Well, Granny, on your way to the Pure Land?"
The woman smiled and nodded.
"I expect Amida is there waiting for you," said the monk.
The woman shook her head violently, looking puzzled.
"If he's not in the Pure Land then where is he?" the monk asked.
The woman looked at him pityingly, tapped her heart three times and
went on her way.
The monk admitted defeat, saying, "There goes a true Pure Land
devotee."

Several other discoveries helped my transition from Zen to the Pure Land tradition though in fact I never actually left Zen behind. One discovery was that the essential practice is in our everyday lives and that the important thing is the remembrance of the Buddha, not the external forms. This practice of simply remembering the Buddha can be done anywhere and at any time. It also includes the practice of inward listening, as it is believed that the impulse to recite the Name comes from the Buddha Amitabha himself.

Everything came to a head when I met a teacher who was both a Pure Land priest and a Zen roshi. Roshi Tairyu Furukawa, who died as this book was being written, was the head priest of the Seimeizan Schweitzer Ji. To find a Buddhist tradition that included the name of Albert Schweitzer in its title was enough to alert me to the fact that here was no ordinary teacher. In his work for some prisoners who had been wrongly found guilty he met with a Protestant leader in Tokyo. When this man died, he left Roshi a relic of Albert Schweitzer, with the request to venerate it. Roshi was so impressed that he enshrined it in his new temple, and it became a part of his tradition.

Roshi Furukawa was also a master calligrapher who had had exhibitions throughout Japan, and in Italy and Poland. He did not speak English, but his daughter Sayuri and his son Ryuji translated very well. However, such was my empathy with him that I could often understand him before the translation was given (and this was not because of my understanding of Japanese, which is non-existent). He taught me a great deal by his presence as well as his words.

Roshi was an extraordinary teacher. He managed to combine Zen and Pure Land approaches in his everyday life with an attitude of service to the world, and work for interfaith harmony. He taught meditation, was a tireless worker for causes of peace and reconciliation, and did not see Pure Land and Zen practice in opposition to each other. These were all aspects of my own life, and he understood this, and encouraged me in them all. A couple of years before he died, he gave me the greatest encouragement of all by ordaining me as a priest in his tradition.

The main thing about Pure Land teaching is that the Buddha accepts us just as we are. One of my favorite poems is by Zuiken:

▶ *Just as you are—*
   Really,
      Just as you are!

Here is the essence of acceptance. As we are completely accepted by the Infinite, just as we are at any moment, so we learn to accept ourselves. This is tremendously liberating because when we are faced with all the stories of the Buddha and other great souls, it is possible to feel inadequate. In fact, if we are honest we *know* we are inadequate. However, when this inadequacy is accepted, we know that "just as we are" we are even now in the Pure Land, and we can relax and live our lives with gratitude and compassion as fully as we can. We may even have glimpses of the Pure Land here and now, not as visions, but as a subtle feeling of wholeness.

Another of the great Pure Land Masters, Ippen Shonin, had a revelation that he was to encourage all beings to say the Nembutsu at least once. He had been traveling throughout Japan encouraging people to say the Name, but requiring a declaration of faith from them. However, this revelation from a manifestation of Amida Buddha requested that they should say it even if they did not have faith. From then on, his teaching was also, "Just say it."

> ❯ *Just say it,*
> *And see what happens.*
>
> *What happens is not your concern.*
> *It is the Power of the Vow Of Amida Buddha.*
> *It is the action of the Great Compassion itself.*
>
> *Just say it,*
> *Perhaps ten times,*
> *Maybe three,*
> *Or even just once.*
>
> *Once may be enough.*
> *If once is enough, then ten times will also be enough,*
> *Or it may be that you want to go on saying it throughout your life,*
> *Until it moves from your head into your heart*
> *And becomes an integral part of your being.*
>
> *Just say it (as many times as you like)*
>
> *Namo Amida Buddha*
> *Namo Amida Buddha*
> *Namo Amida Buddha . . .*

"Namo" is ourselves, and "Amida Buddha" is the Infinite Light of Wisdom and the Life of Compassion. In "Namo Amida Buddha" myself and Amida become one. Then myself disappears, all is Buddha, and all becomes one. For me this is the true mystical teaching of the Dharma.

The Eternal Feminine—
Kwan Yin and Tara

✦

Pure and spotless Radiance
Dark-dispelling Sun.
Compassionate without measure
We call on you.

—THE LOTUS SUTRA

One of the problems that has beset Buddhism in the West is the perception that what we have received from the East has been largely masculine in its teaching and teachers. This has caused some difficulty for women, who have suffered from a male-oriented Christian church for nearly two thousand years. The feminine in spirituality has essential differences, and today women are seeking to express them in ways that will make them feel valued and nurtured. This is important not just for women. It is also vital for men. Buddhism as a whole needs the feminine to have equal expression within the Dharma.

The Buddha lived at a time when the attitude to women was one of ownership, and he actually did much to break down this attitude. Although he was reluctant to allow women to be ordained, this was largely because of the prejudice that he knew would occur as soon as he had left the scene. He was right. This attitude still largely prevails within orthodox Buddhism. However, there is no reason— apart from tradition and culture—why it should, and many women and men are working to ensure that such attitudes do not become a part of Western Buddhism.

It is said that the order of nuns died out in some Buddhist traditions. To enable a valid ordination of nuns to take place, it is necessary for a certain number of ordained nuns to be present. The story goes that at some time the number had so diminished that this was not possible. There are moves today by some nuns to re-create the valid succession by using nuns from the Chinese Sangha in Taiwan, where the traditional ordination of nuns has continued unbroken. A number of nuns from Sri Lankan and Tibetan orders have received this ordination, but it remains to be seen whether it will be widely accepted by the establishment of their native countries.

At a meeting of Western Dharma teachers presided over by the Dalai Lama, one woman teacher painted an elaborate visualization of a possible scenario where the Buddha and all the major teachers were female, and where a solitary male monk was unable to find ways to express his own spirituality in terms that could be understood. This moved His Holiness to tears, and he said that he would call a meeting of all the senior Tibetan abbots to see what could be done. True to his word, he did so, but I gather little came of it.

Some schools of Buddhism, particularly in the West, still have valid orders of nuns, and teachers who are female. In others, such as the Japanese Jodoshinshu, priests can be either male or female. There is no question of gender in the teachings of the essential emptiness of all phenomena, and Buddha Nature is beyond the differences of gender. Also, three of the most popular Bodhisattvas are *Kwan Yin* and *Tara*, the female incarnations of compassion, and *Mahaprajnaparamita*, the female incarnation of wisdom.

I cannot remember when I first saw an image of Kwan Yin. It was probably one of those well-known ones in white porcelain that are found in museums or in Chinese gift shops. In common with many Buddhists, I expect that I had some idea about "the Goddess of Compassion" without fully realizing that she was an integral part of Chinese Buddhist thought and practice. I think it was around 1965 when I obtained my first image of her, a delicately carved wooden figure with features of great compassion, standing on a wide-eyed dragon and holding in her hand the vase of "sweet dew," the nectar of wisdom and compassion. I still have this image, and it has pride of place on my shrine. However, I knew very little about her until the publication in 1977 of John Blofeld's book, *Compassion Yoga: The Mystical Cult of Kuan Yin.*[5]

It is amazing what a great impact this book had on some Western Buddhists, myself among them. It was like finding a whole new aspect of something that we thought we knew well. At that time many people were exploring the native British pre-Christian traditions, including their worship of the Goddess. This may have prepared our minds for this new teaching. The main thing was that it brought the feminine into Buddhism, adding something that we knew was missing, though we were not sure what.

Kwan Yin is the Chinese female form of the Bodhisattva *Avalokiteshvara*, "Regarder of the Cries of the World." She has promised to manifest in whatever form is needed by suffering beings, and Avalokiteshvara is known in various forms—male and female—in different Buddhist traditions. The Dalai Lama is considered a manifestation of Chenrezig, the Tibetan form of Avalokiteshvara. In China she is usually portrayed in the form of a beautiful woman with flowing robes and a compassionate expression on her face.

There are a number of legends as to how this form came to be. She is identified with a princess called Miao Shan, or with Niang Niang, the Heavenly Mother of the Taoist Pantheon. True to her promise, Kwan Yin's following is more than Buddhist as she is accepted as a goddess within both Taoism and Confucianism.

All these stories are quite consistent with the record of her in the *Lotus Sutra*, where she makes a vow that she will take whatever form is necessary to save living beings from suffering. In the twenty-fifth chapter, the Buddha is asked how Avalokiteshvara got her name. He replies that all beings who call her name will be heard and saved by her. Even if there are millions of them, she will be able to deliver them from their trials. He gives examples such as fire, flood, drowning and attack by bandits or demons. He also tells of the various forms in which she can manifest, including that of a Buddha, Bodhisattva, monk, nun, layman, laywoman, animal, deva or other heavenly being. Nowhere does it specify that the form is to be Asian, or even Buddhist. Whatever is necessary is possible. The Buddha also refers specifically to the Bodhisattva's power to grant children to those who pray to her, one of the reasons for her great popularity in China.

Devotion to Kwan Yin became a regular part of the group practice of the Pure Land Buddhist Fellowship. Many of us regularly chant her mantra, "Namo Kwan Shih Yin Pu Sa," in our daily practice. Many experiences brought home to us the reality of Kwan Yin's presence. There were healings of mind and body as well as some that might be called coincidences, but too many for us not to find something significant in them.

I know of one man who was standing by a bus stop in central London. Suddenly, he felt moved to recite Kwan Yin's mantra, but did not know why. Without warning, a woman pushing a pram headed out into the road. A car, accelerating away from traffic, roared towards her and her baby. My friend could do nothing, and just kept repeating the mantra. Miraculously, the car managed to stop in a space that could not have been more than about ten yards. My friend is convinced that this was due to Kwan Yin's intervention.

One of the chief blessings that Kwan Yin brings into our lives is a reminder of the peace and stillness that is the essence of our Buddha-Nature. One member of our Buddhist group has an image of her in every room, and says just having her form within sight is a great help in maintaining equilibrium in difficult circumstances. Others have images of her in the garden, and report that this too brings peace. She is truly the universal manifestation of the Great Compassion, and she does not deny her blessings to anyone who calls on her, by whatever name. Some even see her in the form of the Christian Mary, the Mother of God.

It is said that the female Buddha Tara was born of a tear shed by Avalokiteshvara for the suffering of the world. Tara has all the qualities of compassion of Kwan Yin, yet is in many ways more human. She is a very powerful being, and as the Mother of all the Buddhas, is seen as the source of all their strength, and the eternal fount of their Compassion. She also manifests in a number of different forms, in which color is one of the principal differences, and she can even appear in wrathful form to give her devotees the power to overcome those who would do harm to them or to the Dharma.

One particular legend, tells how, many ages ago, Tara was a woman called Wisdom Moon, a devotee of the Drum Sound Buddha. Over many years, she worshiped this Buddha and made offerings. One day, when she felt the time was right, she took the Bodhisattva Vow in the presence of the Buddha, promising to attain enlightenment in order to benefit all beings. The monks rejoiced at this, and advised her to pray that she would be reborn as a man, which they said would make the attainment of enlightenment easier.

Wisdom Moon was distressed by their attitude, and pointed out that she had gone beyond gender. As there were few women known to follow the path, she said that, "As long as this world is not freed from suffering, I will benefit beings by appearing in a woman's body." The strength of her practice allowed her to realize the ultimate truth, and her *samadhi* enabled her to achieve the state where she became known as "The Savioress" or Tara in Sanskrit. Her main activity is to help beings overcome fear and danger, and it is said that every day she liberates an infinite number. Tara dwells in her own Pure Land called "The Harmony of Turquoise Leaves."

Tara has many devotees among Western Buddhists, many of whom have stories to tell about her. A friend came across a large image of Tara in the British Museum. As he was looking at the image, what he described as a bolt of electricity passed though him, and he seemed for a timeless moment to become one with the image. He saw a vision of a shrine room with a smaller image on the shrine, and he knew that he had to find out more. Many years later, when he had become a devotee of Tara, he went to a Buddhist center to hear a talk, and recognized the room from his vision.

After my first experience of meeting Tara, it seemed as if she came on the scene through many different means. I met a number of people who were devotees, and who spoke of her in terms that were both reverent and friendly. However, I did not have an image of her that had real meaning for me. Then, through good fortune, I heard that His Holiness the Dalai Lama was to give the Green Tara empowerment in London. Although I was not practicing any of the Tibetan forms of Buddhism, I felt that I had to go.

Empowerment, or initiation, is a ceremony that has several levels. For the serious practitioner, it fertilizes their practice and enables it to proceed to its final goal of liberation. For them, it is necessary not only to have the empowerment, but also the teachings that enable this blessing to be used to its fullest extent. For others, the term "blessing" is indeed appropriate. It is a means through that the compassionate grace of the Buddha is shared with those who receive it. This is what I felt I needed.

I attended the empowerment with about five hundred other people, and it was an interesting occasion. With my deep regard for His Holiness and my love for Tara I had been expecting a sublime spiritual experience. I wish I could say that it was, but it wasn't. I am sure that the fault was mine. It was, as I have said, interesting. Nothing else happened for some time. Seeds need time to germinate in dark- ness, and without particularly intending to, I did the right thing: I left them alone. One of my teachers was very fond of using garden- ing metaphors for the spiritual life, and I had been told many years before that if you want good flowers, you don't keep digging up the seeds to see how they are growing. It is good advice for anyone on the spiritual path.

Several years later my wife and I were in northern California, and happened to pass a shop selling high-quality Tibetan arts and crafts. I had a sudden urge to go in and ask if they had a represen- tation of Green Tara, even though reason told me that it would be more than I could afford. They checked through their stock, but did not have one. However, the shop was connected with a Buddhist Center some miles away, and telephoned to see if they had one. They had two, so we followed the directions and arrived at the center. We were greeted by the lama in charge, who turned out to be the son of a well-known incarnate lama who had written a book on Tara. They made us welcome, and showed us the *thankas* (wall hangings). Though they were beautiful pieces I did not like either of them, and they were much too expensive.

We carried on with our tour, and eventually came to Shasta City. Shasta is a little like Glastonbury in England, with many eso- teric organizations and bookshops. We visited a bookshop that we knew from a previous visit, didn't find anything we wanted, and started to leave. Then I had the most strange experience. As I was going out the front door I literally found myself walking backwards into the shop again and heading towards the back. There, on the wall, was the most exquisite tiny thanka of Green Tara, about six inches by five, mounted on dark green silk framed with yellow. The price was easily affordable, and I bought it. It hangs on my office wall to the side of my shrine as I type this, and I will always consider it a gift from Tara herself. Later, I was to find a similar White Tara in a shop in the heart of Dublin, and that too is on my wall. Both seem to smile as I tell this story.

There is nothing unusual in this story. Many devotees of Tara, Kwan Yin and the Virgin Mary tell of similar happenings in their lives. The feminine Principle of Compassion, by whatever name, brings blessings to us in ways that might seem trivial, except that they always seem to have an impact on our spiritual lives. There is no way of knowing why this should happen, or who will be the recipients of such grace. We can only be grateful for it.

I do not think that for me the story is finished. I am not a practitioner of Tibetan forms of meditation and practice, and I have still not sought the teaching that would enable me to follow this path. I regularly chant Kwan Yin's mantra, and I am grateful to sense the unity between Tara, Kwan Yin and the Christian Virgin Mary to whom I used to pray as a child. I know the teaching that these forms are in essence manifestations of the Infinite Mind, but I cannot yet make the leap that leaves them behind. Maybe I do not have to. Whatever form the feminine spiritual power takes in our lives, it is good to recognize it. As its influence grows, I am conscious of being led gently and compassionately towards the goal, and I await the next stage with interest.

Buddhism and Healing

◆

Don't regard illness as a hindrance, or consider it a virtue
Leave your mind unfabricated and free ...
Cutting through the flow of conceptual thoughts.
Old illnesses will disappear by themselves
And you will remain unharmed by new ones.

—PADMASAMBHAVA, EIGHTH-CENTURY TIBETAN SAGE

Buddhism has a long tradition of healing dating back to the Buddha himself. However, this was more or less forgotten as the generations after Shakyamuni concentrated on rules of organization and practice. This seems to be the pattern in all faiths. In spite of Jesus' injunction that his followers were to "heal the sick and preach the gospel," the first part was overlooked as Christian priests lost the consciousness of healing that Jesus taught. Yet healing could be said to be essential Buddhism, because the Buddha's teaching about the "The Way out of suffering" is healing in its truest, most complete, spiritual sense. Today, many spiritual healers are Buddhists, and find that their faith in no way conflicts with their healing practice.

In the Pali Canon the Buddha talks repeatedly about the causes of suffering, and the practices whereby we can eliminate them. One is to meditate on what is called "the seven limbs of enlightenment." These are: mindfulness, profound inquiry into the nature of Dharma, vigor, joy, tranquillity, deep meditation and equanimity. Meditation on these is the way to overcome the poisons of lust, anger and delusion, which directly relate to the physical causes of illness, excesses of wind, bile and phlegm.

There are several cases of healing through these seven limbs recorded in the Pali Canon.

▶ *Once, the elder Kassapa was ill, and the Buddha visited him. Kassapa asked the Buddha whether he could help.*

The Buddha spoke about the seven limbs, saying:

"Kassapa, these are the seven limbs of enlightenment which I have fully expounded and taught. Meditate and think on them, and they will lead to a full understanding, to Nirvana."

On hearing these words, Kassapa was immediately healed of his sickness, and rose up and served the Buddha.

Once the Buddha himself was sick, and asked a disciple to repeat the seven limbs to him to bring about healing. From this and other examples it is clear that enlightenment was seen by the Buddha as related to the healing of body and mind. From the Buddhist point of view, all suffering—including sickness—comes from a false view of the world. This view is maya or illusion. If we can see through this to the world as it really is, then we know that we, like everything else, are subject to change. This change can be influenced in a positive way. It is hard for us to see this in the suffering world in which we live, particularly if we are in pain. Nonetheless, if we can see through this illusion of the world—and the illusion of the self who observes it—then the truth of things as they are can emerge, and healing results.

This belief is similar to that employed in some Western forms of healing, such as Christian Science. Buddhist healing is more than just the cure of an illness. It directly involves the turning around of a person's life and thought. Jesus often used a term that has been translated as "repent!" but actually means "change your minds" (or your way of thinking). The well-known healer and author Walter Lanyon wrote:

> ▶ *When you see God in a patient*
> *You bring forth what is called a healing;*
> *But in Reality you do nothing*
> *But recognize a fact of being.*[6]

Substitute the Three Signs of Being for God, and you have the essence of the Buddhist approach to healing.

I remember one of my teachers used to meet every circumstance with the saying, "This too will pass." He advised us to do the same. Though not a Buddhist, in this he was very close to Buddhist teaching. This is applicable to both good and bad times. We do not really know what is good and what is bad. A well-known Christian hymn sums it up well.

> ▶ *Those dark clouds that ye so much dread,*
> *Shall break in blessing on your head.*

The following story, though Taoist in origin, is also told in Buddhist circles.

> ▶ *An elderly farmer had a beautiful horse. One day it ran away. His neighbors came to commiserate with him on his loss, but all he said was, "Who knows what's good; who knows what's bad."*
>
> *The horse returned, bringing with it several wild horses, and his neighbors came to congratulate him on his good fortune. All he said was, "Who knows what's good; who knows what's bad."*
>
> *His son started to train the wild horses, but one of them threw him and he broke his leg. His neighbors came to sympathize with the farmer, but all he said was, "Who knows what's good; who knows what's bad."*

The Emperor's army marched through the district, press-ganging every young man into service, but they did not take the farmer's son, as he had a broken leg. The farmer's comment was still, "Who knows what's good; who knows what's bad."

The practice of metta or loving-kindness (see page 64) also relates to healing. This practice, whether to others or oneself, is not performed idly. I truly believe it has a beneficial effect on the world and on individuals. I know many people who do this meditation every day for those who ask for it, with surprising and occasionally miraculous results. Loving-kindness and compassion really do influence change in a positive direction.

Metta is also important in the realm of self-healing. To wish ourselves well is to really love ourselves, and this is something that few people in the West seem to be able to do. We have been brought up to feel that to love ourselves is selfish, but in fact it is the reverse. Only if we truly love ourselves can we love others. "Love thy neighbor *as thyself*" is the true teaching of Christ *and* Buddha.

There are Cosmic Buddhas and Bodhisattvas who are specifically involved in healing. In particular, there is the Buddha called Lapis Lazuli Radiance Medicine Buddha, or *Bhaisajya Guru*, The Master of Healing. This Buddha also created a Buddha-land and made vows to help suffering beings. His vows include the emitting of radiant healing lights, helping beings to obtain the necessities of life, healing through the power of his name those who are sick or deformed, and helping all beings to become enlightened. He also undertook to contain all the poisons of the world, and to purify them into the Lapis Lazuli healing light that would be emitted from his body.

The practice with this Buddha involves visualizing his radiant blue form, chanting his name and meditating on the pure blue light that is the manifestation of his healing compassion. It is interesting that this blue light is the one favored for healing by contemporary

healers who practice color treatment. For those who find such visualization easy, it is said that holding oneself and others in the clear
blue light of this Buddha is a very potent way of healing.

> ▶ *Sit quietly, and breathe gently to calm the mind.*
> *Do not expect to make the mind a blank.*
> *Just breathe gently and relax, watching the breath.*
>
> *Imagine a Buddha figure, sitting or standing.*
> *His body is pure blue lapis lazuli.*
> *Concentrate on the color, until you lose the form.*
>
> *Now feel that the color is everywhere.*
> *It is here in your own body.*
> *It is warm, gentle, soothing.*
> *As you breathe,*
> *Become aware of its reaching every cell in your body and mind.*
> *Feel at one with the Pure Blueness.*
>
> *Now, make the intention to share this with those who are sick.*
> *See the pure blue light reaching out to them*
> *Shining in the space where they are.*
> *Hold each one in this light for a minute or so, silently reciting their*
> *names.*
>
> *When you have finished,*
> *See the light form back into the Buddha figure.*
> *Join your palms prayerwise,*
> *And give thanks.*

Some say that any approach to the spiritual healing of illness is going
against the teaching of karma. If this were true all forms of medical
healing would also be doing so. Manifesting compassion never goes
against our karma, but creates good karma that transforms it. Whatever approach you take to Buddhist practice, including meditation,

remember that the Buddha taught the Dharma as "the Way out of suffering." Anything that contributes towards this goal is true Dharma.

One specifically Buddhist form of healing relates to those who become ill though the practice of intense meditation. I have met many people who suffer from ill-health caused by this. This so-called "meditation sickness" is fairly common, and takes many forms. Symptoms can include severe headaches, digestive problems, backache, problems with energy and the immune system, and all those related to stress and tension. This illness can be very serious and debilitating. Meditation is supposed to be a help in finding the way out of suffering, so these strange side-effects are often not associated in the mind of the meditator with the excesses of spiritual discipline.

People forget that meditation is not just something you do, and think that the harder they try, the sooner they will be enlightened. We do have to do our best, the Buddha told us, but something else is necessary. In the Buddha's day people were often enlightened just by hearing the Buddha speak. Many of the great masters since the Buddha's time were enlightened when they had given up trying or were relaxing and not thinking about enlightenment.

Hakuin Zenji, the great reformer of Zen, writes of just such an experience in his book *Yasenkanna*.[7] He had become a monk at a very young age, and studied with a number of the greatest masters of the time. He pushed himself harder and harder, and even had a flash of enlightenment, but was still not satisfied, and eventually became very ill. He managed to find his way to an adept who lived in solitude in the mountains. He gave Hakuin some simple breathing and visualization exercises that helped to restore him to full health and vitality.

These healing exercises consist of instructions to relax deeply, to count the breaths up to one hundred and to practice a form of visualization. Imagine a ball of Celestial Healing Cream above the head. This cream is visualized as the essence of purity, and is a gift from Heaven. Though it is a mental creation, it has the wonderful prop-

erty of being able to dissolve and flow downwards through the physical body, relaxing, easing, soothing and healing all that it touches.

> ▶ *Lie down somewhere comfortable, and be sure you are warm.*
> *Relax, and breathe slowly and gently, counting the breath up to one*
> *hundred.*
> *Do not worry if you miscount; just start again from where you think*
> *you have got to, or go back to the beginning.*
>
> *Next, imagine this ball of Celestial Healing Cream, shining brightly*
> *above your head.*
> *In your imagination, allow it to melt, moving slowly downwards*
> *through your body.*
>
> *Feel it flow down through the head and face,*
> *the neck and shoulders,*
> *the chest and back,*
> *the arms to the hands,*
> *the diaphragm and stomach,*
> *down through the lower abdomen, the hips, thighs*
> *and legs to the feet.*
> *As it flows, it soothes and pacifies each part of the body.*
>
> *Next become aware of it accumulating in the lower abdomen [two*
> *fingers below the navel]*
> *And resting there, from where it is a source of energy and peace.*
> *Let your mind rest there, and be aware of your gentle breathing.*
> *Abide in this relaxed peace, and rest [for as long as you like].*

If you have been striving hard at meditation practice and are feeling
unwell, stressed or tense, it may be that you are suffering from something like this meditation sickness. Do not blame yourself for your
state, and do not blame anyone else either. Learn to relax deeply, go
for walks, or take up some form of artistic activity; do anything but

strive for spiritual progress. However much we try we cannot tell how we are progressing, and trying too hard is definitely counter-productive.

People also have problems because they strive for experiences. The Buddha teaches that meditation need not lead to experiences, and that we should avoid seeking them. Phenomena such as seeing visions, lights and colors, and feelings of warmth or power may happen, but they are not to be regarded as significant, and certainly not to be striven for. If they occur we are advised to note them without involvement, and they will go away as they came.

The real fruit of meditation is healing. It is a subtle change that is hardly noticeable at first. It gently permeates your life, helping you to live in harmony with yourself and others. This is the real experience. Stay with it, and all will be clear.

The Circle of Compassion

◆

The salvation
Of birds and beasts, oneself included—
This is the object
Of Shakyamuni's religious austerities . . .

—IKKYU, TRANS. R. H. BLYTH

*I*n this little verse we have the essence of the original teaching of
Shakyamuni Buddha, and those of his followers who embraced
the homeless life. The verse affirms that compassion was and is the
essence of Buddhism. Some of the teachings we have received in the
West present a slightly austere version of the original teachings. However, the experience of those who have lived in Buddhist countries is
of the immense warmth and compassion of the people in their Buddhist lives and practice.

I remember taking my wife—who is not a Buddhist—to visit
a very senior monk who had become something of a personal friend
(and still is, though I see him very rarely). When we arrived we were
told he was resting but, on hearing our voices, he came out to see who
had arrived and warmly greeted us, shaking hands with us both.
(The rules say monks are not supposed to touch women.) He then
insisted on making us tea and serving us himself, in spite of my ask-

ing that I should be allowed to do it. He joined us for tea and biscuits. When I spoke to him later about the monastic rules, which would seem to have forbidden him from doing all these things, he merely smiled and said, "There is a higher rule than those." "What is that?" I asked. "The rule of hospitality," he replied.

Likewise, I once took a friend who had some problems relating to Tibetan teaching to visit a senior lama who I thought might be able to help. When we were shown into the room he sprang up from his seat, piled cushions against the wall for us, and only after he had been assured that we were comfortable did he resume his seat (which was also on the floor and not raised up in any way) and ask how he could help. His compassionate actions proved to be the gateway through which he was able to help my friend. As she said afterwards, "I was very nervous about going to see him, but he was so kind that all my nerves went, and I felt really in tune with him."

The Dalai Lama is on record as saying, "My religion is kindness." Applying the test of the *Kalama Sutra*, we do not accept this for ourselves because it is written in a book or because a much-respected teacher has said it. We accept it because it is obvious that if we do so then the world becomes a better place. Further, we can accept it not because it is part of a particular tradition, but because it is a universal norm. We have all had experience of the transforming power of kindness. It transforms not only the lives of the people to whom it is directed, but also the life of the person who is being kind. This is the essence of metta meditation, and why the Buddha considered it to be sufficient in itself to guide us to enlightenment.

Some Buddhist teachers have said that kind acts are nothing to do with the quest for enlightenment. Such acts cannot be truly compassionate unless we are enlightened. I do not believe this is so. Roshi Furukawa taught that compassion is an integral part of the teaching of both Zen and Pure Land Buddhism. He told the following story about a master called Kazan, and then commented on it.

❭ *One day the old master was on his round begging for alms, leading his six disciples.*

When they came to an upward slope they saw a cart at a standstill, piled high with a heavy load.

Kato Osho, one of the disciples, left the line without thinking and pushed the back of the cart.

Upon seeing this, the old master immediately turned on his heel and went back to the monastery alone.

He then gave an order through an attendant that Kato should leave the monastery.

Expulsion from the monastery was the ultimate penalty.

Roshi Furukawa commented:

❭ *It could be said that in Zen we address ourselves thoroughly to the study of koan, casting the problem of the cart aside, whereas in the Pure Land tradition, we do Nembutsu while pushing the cart as a koan.*

We might think that a story of such an austere Buddhist practice (refraining from expressions of love such as pushing the cart) seems refreshing, and that this would be the proper image of a Buddhist.

[We would be wrong] . . . If I had been the old master Kazan and had seen the cart, I would have scolded the five remaining disciples who assumed an indifferent attitude towards the cart, towards the reality in front of their very eyes.

Sitting in meditation may be a practice that will eventually save the whole world, but the need for compassionate action is immediate, and needs to be followed through at the time. Once the opportunity for compassion has gone, it can never be recaptured. Compassion is the essence of the practice of living in the now, or mindfulness. It is the great transformer of karma; in fact, it is the only means by which our negative karma can be transformed.

D. T. Suzuki once wrote that those who fail to grasp the true spirit of compassion are unable to grasp the true meaning of religion, be it Christian or Buddhist.[8] Just as the Buddhism that has come to the West has emphasized meditation, and has inspired many Christians to recover this element in their own faith, so has the Christian emphasis on compassion helped Buddhists to rediscover this element. In fact, meditation has never been absent from Christianity, and compassion is the essence of Buddhism. The ideal of Buddhism has always been to rescue all beings from this world of suffering, but we have sometimes overlooked the suffering that is right in front of us.

For me, an important part of my Buddhism is to be a vegetarian, but I recognize that you do not have to be a vegetarian to be a Buddhist. There are many millions of Buddhists who are not vegetarian. Only one of my various teachers was a vegetarian. But when I am asked, "Why are you a vegetarian?" my answer is still, "Because I am a Buddhist." I claim no virtue in being a vegetarian. It just happened. I suppose we should say that it was my karma; I did not make a personal decision. I just gradually developed an aversion to eating meat. Meat began to make me feel sick. People who still love meat have to make the decision to do what their conscience or their personal beliefs tell them. The whole question is summed up in the verse by Ikkyu at the head of this chapter. If the austerities of the Buddha are truly for the salvation of all beings, including birds and beasts, then is it logical that we should eat their bodies?

When I worked for the Vegetarian Society as their London Secretary, I used to be invited to various places to give talks to organizations including the Young Farmers' Clubs. Possibly they thought they would have a good time baiting the speaker. Without fail, at every such talk I was asked, "Do you think that vegetarians are more compassionate than those who look after handicapped children or sick people?" My answer was—and is—definitely, "No!"

Having been caught out on the first couple of occasions, I developed what I still believe is the right answer. I call it "The Circle of Compassion." I am not sure where my answer came from, but I clearly remember the flash of inspiration that came the first time I was asked this question. It so happened that there was a blackboard and chalk available and, though I do not usually use them, I went to the board and drew a circle. "Imagine that this circle is the full three hundred and sixty degrees of possible human compassion. Most of us will manifest ten, twenty or thirty degrees in our lifetime, and it does not matter to me where this is situated on the circle." My answer proved acceptable to the farmers, but not to some of the more extreme vegetarians who felt that only their way was truly compassionate. I still remember the horror it provoked when I included it in a talk to a local vegetarian society. I still believe it is so, but I did learn a valuable lesson in tailoring my response to my audience.

Animals also have qualities of compassion. There are many stories of sacrifice by dogs, but this is one that really made me think.

▶ *A farmer decided that he was going to clear his barn of rats. He used smoke and his dogs to chase the rats out of the stacks of straw. While this was going on, he and several others waited with guns and shot the rats who bolted from the barn. Finally, he had his son drive their small tractor into the stacks to level them.*

After most of the rats had come out and been shot, a rat emerged with a piece of straw in its mouth, at the other end of which was another rat. The farmer shot one rat, whereupon the other, instead of running, just stood still. Intrigued, the farmer walked up to it, but it still stood there and allowed him to throw a bucket over it. He was worried that it might carry some kind of special disease, and so he took it to a Ministry of Agriculture Veterinary Officer, who discovered that the rat was blind. The other rat had been leading it by the straw.

This story changed my attitude to the animal kingdom (though I still don't particularly like rats).

I believe that it is important for each person to make up their own mind what they do towards filling the circle. Some day in the future, we may suddenly find that it is full, and then we will realize that the world is free from suffering. Until then, let each of us do our best.

Words of Power, Words of Peace

◆

Greater than the Big Bang
Smaller than a heartbeat
The Sound of Buddha

—LING CHAO

When I was a child the nuns at my preparatory school used to insist that every time we used the name of "Jesus," we bowed our heads. It was fascinating to discover many years later that this practice was also part of Buddhism, though of course the holy name was "Buddha." We do not know where the practice of reciting the name of Buddha first began, but it is probable that the holy name of "Buddha" was one of the first Buddhist *mantras*.

The practice of mantra within Buddhism goes back to the early years. Many of the Mahayana scriptures include mantras or *dharanis*. A dharani is more or less a long mantra. It is also translated as "spell," but, given the Buddha's teachings about magic, I do not feel that this can be correct. However, millions of Buddhists use mantras and dharanis as spells to ward off evil and bring good fortune.

The real purpose of a mantra is to help the person using it to make contact with other levels of reality, particularly those that are helpful in the quest for enlightenment. John Blofeld calls them "sacred words of power."[9] Many mantras are only given in secret while others, though widely known, are said to be effective only if accompanied by secret yogic practices.

This is all right for those who are studying seriously with a qualified teacher, but there are mantras that are freely available to everyone. They are in many ways similar to prayers such as the Jesus Prayer of the Orthodox Church, "Lord Jesus Christ, have mercy on me," or the Muslim "Allah is Great." In the Hindu tradition, with which the Buddha must have been familiar, there are names of God that can be used by anyone, but they are said to have enhanced power when transmitted through initiation by a teacher who has experienced their ability to lead to realization. There are also "hidden names," which are known only to initiates.

A contemporary example of this is the initiation of the Transcendental Meditation movement in which those who are initiated are specifically told to keep the mantra a secret. I have noticed that even those who have left the movement and no longer practice TM are still reluctant to tell the mantra to others. In contrast to this, the Hare Krishna movement broadcasts its Maha Mantra

> *Hare Krishna, Hare Krishna,*
> *Krishna Krishna, Hare Hare,*
> *Hare Rama, Hare Rama,*
> *Rama Rama, Hare Hare*

as widely as possible, and encourages everybody to chant it.

The *Ji* school of Buddhism in Japan encouraged everyone to chant the Nembutsu at least once, believing that it was their duty to ensure that all were saved. They also distributed amulets of the Nembutsu, and recorded the names of those who were "saved." This last practice led to conflict within their movement and it lost many mem-

bers to the more popular Jodoshinshu, eventually becoming a rela-
tively minor tradition in Japanese Buddhism.

One of the first Buddhist mantras that I came across was the
well-known "Om Mani Padme Hum." I have found it used as a chant,
a meditation, before zazen and in connection with healing work. It
is also connected with Kwan Yin, and has links with the Tibetan tradition and the Dalai Lama. I have found its use very helpful at times
of great difficulty in my life. Lama Govinda has written a whole book
about its meaning and use, which is too complex to quote here.[10]
Another more simple meaning was given to me many years ago by a
Hindu swami who said that it had been given to him by a Tibetan
Yogi he had met in India. This meaning emphasizes the mantra's uni-
versality, and rings true to me as a mystical interpretation.

> **Om**—this is the Infinite in the Sanskrit tongue (from which this
> mantra originally comes). It is said to be the creative sound, from which
> comes all grace and blessing.
> **Mani Padme**—this is the Sanskrit for "Jewel in the Lotus," which is a
> synonym for the human heart.
> **Hum**—this is the relative world; this suffering world, samsara.

On the relative plane, this mantra is a way of drawing blessings from
the Infinite, processing them (as it were) through the human heart
and sending them out to the world. It is the mantra of compassion.
On the mystical level, it is living proof of the Buddhist saying that
in reality *nirvana* and *samsara* are one. While we think of nirvana and
samsara we are still in the world of duality, but the Mani takes us
beyond this into realization of the Oneness of all.

I have also been told that the mantra has links with Jesus Christ,
who was supposed to have visited India and Tibet, and so is a way of
unifying Christian roots with the Buddhist life. I have no proof that
this is true, but I feel intuitively that it might be. My feeling comes

from the experience of a remarkable peace when I recite it in a Christian church, where it seems to provide a link with Jesus.

It does not seem to be important that we pronounce the mantra correctly. It has different pronunciations when used in its Sanskrit, Chinese or Tibetan form. A story from the Orthodox Christian tradition exemplifies this, even thought it is told more in terms of prayer.

▶ *There were three old hermits living on an island. Each day they prayed to the Holy Trinity, "You are Three, we are three, bless us."*

One day, the local bishop visited the island, and asked what practices the hermits used. They told him that they prayed in this way.

The bishop was horrified, and told them that they must stop and use one of the formal prayers of the Church. As the hermits could not read, he taught them a prayer.

It was late evening when the bishop left, and as his boat traveled away from the island, he congratulated himself on a job well done.

Suddenly, a light was seen chasing the boat, and the three hermits appeared running on the water. The boat stopped, and when they caught up they said to the bishop, "We have forgotten your prayer, please teach us."

The bishop humbly told them, "Go back and pray, 'You are Three, we are three, bless us,' and remember me in your prayers."

A contemporary approach has been within the realm of scientific research. The Transcendental Meditation people have researched the psycho-physical effects of mantra meditation. Inspired by this, other scientists have experimented in the use of a suitable word repeated slowly in the same way. Words such as "peace," "joy," "patience," etc., have been used and the results monitored in terms of brainwaves, circulation, pulse and other physical effects. Checks on the psychological state of the meditators have found that regular meditators develop the quality of the word they are using, becoming more peaceful and less liable to angry reactions. The overall state of their health also improved, particularly in relation to diseases associated with stress.

Some Buddhists are skeptical of such practices. They feel that the concentration on physical and psychological effects detracts from the true spiritual purpose of the mantra. This may or may not be true, but the Buddha was definitely interested in these factors in his "way out of suffering." He may have been all-seeing, beyond time and infinite in wisdom and knowledge, but I do wonder if he was able to foresee the problems associated with living in the modern Western world, with all its differences from the world in which he lived.

For example, many of us need to develop patience. I know that I do. Eastern audiences are able to sit for five or six hours on the floor listening to an Indian sitar concert or watching a Japanese *no* play, but few Westerners can do so. If we have a concert—even of music we love—that lasts three hours, we usually need a break in the middle. The stress of a difficult and responsible job often has ramifications that stretch far beyond ourselves, and the burden of responsibility for home, family, fellow workers and even social status often proves too much and leads to burn-out. We live in a far more complex society than that of India in the time of the Buddha, and there are no signs that it will get less. The instant access of computers and the internet will add to it, while the increasing number of leisure distractions, which are called relaxing, may be the reverse. Nothing can take the place of the relaxed state of meditation where body and mind are truly rested.

Easing the suffering caused by stress can lead to a realization that, if what the Buddha taught is able to help, then the other things that he said might well also be true. Back to the Four Noble Truths and the Eightfold Path! In addition in this world of advertising pressure, might not a consideration of the wisdom of the *Kalama Sutra* prove helpful to us all?

▶ *Sit quietly in a chair for a few minutes, watching your breathing.*

Remember that this is not a breathing exercise. You are not trying to change it.
Then think to yourself what quality you might need to develop, such as love, peace, patience etc.
Repeat the word slowly and silently to yourself.
Think about what it means, or picture an example of it.
Do not try to match the repetition to your breathing, but notice how this will happen naturally.
Do not strain in any way.
Do not do it for too long at first, ten minutes should be enough.
Try to do it morning and evening.
Allow the time to grow naturally if it will.

In moments of stress, you can repeat the word a few times, and it will help you to peace and clarity.
Take a number of such breaks throughout your working day.

Watch the results.
If it works for you, then keep at it,
changing the word from time to time as necessary.
If after a month, it does not seem to work, then try something else.

Either way, do not be hard on yourself.

The experience of many people through the ages, not only within Buddhism, is that mantras have a power and a peace that we can tap into by using them correctly. As we learn to contact the heart of the mantra, and allow the mantra into our hearts, then its essence can work in our lives. If we find the right one for us, and practice regularly, the possibilities are endless.

Rocking-Chair Meditation

✦

Old Rocking Chair:
My slowest boat
To China.

—LING CHAO

Many years ago I came across a book that advocated using a rocking chair for meditation. I do not think that the book was Buddhist, and the title of it escapes my memory. In fact, I do not remember much about the book nor even the type of meditation that it proposed. It was just this one idea, "rocking-chair meditation," that stuck in my mind.

Probably one of the reasons why this idea stayed with me was that one of my first teachers had left me a rocking chair in her will. I still have it, and I do use it for meditation. Usually I just sit in it. There is something about rocking chairs that helps the mind to become naturally still. The only effort you have to use is the slight movement of rocking. Even this soon becomes completely natural and effortless, and the mind can drift with the rhythm.

My rocking chair is placed in front of a beautiful Tibetan thanka of Chenrezig, one of the forms of Avalokiteshvara. The combination of gentle rocking and the warmth and beauty of the painting combine to bring me to a state of deep meditation without any of the usual barriers. This does not always work, but when it does it is something quite beautiful and unique.

The rhythm of a rocking chair is suitable for reciting a mantra or short prayer. After a while it becomes perfectly natural and you do not have to give it any thought. Because of the painting of Chenrezig, I use the Mani Mantra or sometimes the Nembutsu, but you can use any mantra or prayer that has meaning for you. One of the most important elements of mantra that is often overlooked is rhythm and the use of the rocking chair brings out this aspect. Rhythm becomes more than just an activity of the mind, as the gentle movement of the chair involves the whole body. This adds a new and different dimension to the meditation, and is so pleasurable that it seems to ask for further practice.

Even without the mantra, the gentle rhythm of the chair is a great help to the meditative state of mind. Dogen, the founder of the Soto school of Zen Buddhism, encouraged his disciples to "just sit" in zazen, without any effort to do anything else.

> ▶ *An old man used to sit for hours on his rocking chair on the veranda of his house.*
> *His young nephew asked him one day what he did there.*
> *"Sometimes," he said, "I sits and thinks.*
> *And sometimes I just sits."*

Meditation in a rocking chair is a bit like both.

You might ask, "What has this to do with Buddhism?" The answer is probably nothing, but it does have a lot to do with Dharma. Dharma is the discovery of the naturalness of life, and there are few better vehicles to do this than a good rock on a old, reliable chair. It feels like a chariot that carries its user to realms that are at the same time beyond this world and right here and now. Mindfulness is natural in a rocking chair, but at the same time the rhythm and comfortable feeling combine to transport us beyond our usual consciousness.

If part of Western Buddhism is to discover the Dharma in our everyday lives, then I am sure that rocking chairs will have a role in the future. A good rocking chair is so ordinary, and yet it reminds us of an extraordinary state of mind which, if not already enlightened, is certainly on the way.

The Way On

You Are Born Where You Are Born— Karma and Rebirth

◆

In life or death
with the Buddha
the journey continues.

—ZUIKEN

One of the things that people think they know about Buddhism is that it requires us to believe in karma and reincarnation. The trouble is that it doesn't. As we have seen, Buddhist teaching is something that you take, practice and accept or reject. Belief does not come into it. Anyway, the Buddha's teaching concerns rebirth and not reincarnation.

Reincarnation is the teaching that the soul or spirit leaves one body at death and enters into another one at conception or birth. The Buddha taught that all is constant change, with no separate fixed entity that can be called "a soul." Instead, there are the ever-changing skandhas or constituents of being. The constant interplay of these determines who, what and where a new birth will be. As form is one of these skandhas, rebirth will always take place in some kind of form. The number of shapes that this form can take is potentially infinite, and beyond speculation. All depends on the interplay between the skandhas at the moment of passing.

Life is continuous. There is no concept of creation within Buddhism, so there is no beginning. Some say that nirvana is an ending, but the Buddha would not say what actually happens. In the Bodhisattva teaching of the Mahayana tradition, it is quite clear that if there is an ending it will only happen when there are no beings anywhere who suffer. It goes on to say that all is emptiness, and no one, not even the Buddha, is ever born. Therefore in reality there is no death or rebirth.

Karma is the influence that the activities of our lives, including thoughts and emotions, have on the relationship of our skandhas. It is from a root meaning "action," and is extended to mean "the result of action," in other words, "cause and effect." All actions from this and previous lives can have an effect on this life. Karma is usually seen in respect of good karma and bad karma, but there is much more. There is family karma, national karma, a still wider karma caused by our being human and probably other levels that we cannot even begin to imagine.

Karma is far more than just a simple philosophy of "As you sow, so shall you reap." Even if you accept the idea of karma, simple concepts such as someone being born disabled because of sins in a past life are judgmental and best avoided. Even a simple relationship here in this present life is incredibly complex. Think of the difficulties in relationships where, as the teaching goes, every living being may have been your mother, father, sister, brother, friend or enemy. You have to admit that such judgements are beyond the human mind.

Within most religious traditions that accept karma, there is a being who determines the balance of good and bad in our lives, and authorizes our future incarnation. Buddhism knows no such being. It is we ourselves who influence the skandhas, and our new birth is determined by ourselves as we obey or otherwise the laws of life. It is our intention that is most important in determining our karmic future.

Leaving aside for a moment any questions of Buddhist metaphysics and the nature of life and matter, the question of our birth in this life is one that has important ramifications for Buddhist practice. We are born as we are, and we have to make the most of it. If the Buddhist ideas of karma and rebirth are correct, then there are reasons why we are born in a certain body, in a specific place, to particular parents and into a Western culture. We can never fully understand exactly why such an event occurs—at least, not until we are fully enlightened—so I am not going to speculate. However, the process must involve our relationships with people and places, concepts of responsibility, and the need to learn certain lessons.

The following stories may help to illustrate that it is not wise to judge another person's life in terms of a simple concept of karma.

▶ *An old man used to attend the lectures of the Zen Master Hyakujo. However, when the monks tried to ask who the old man was or why he was there, he mysteriously disappeared. One day, the master himself came down from his seat at the end of his talk, and asked him, "Who are you, and why are you here?" "Dismiss the monks, and I will tell you," said the old man.*

After the master had dismissed the monks, the man replied, "In spite of appearances, I am not human. Many years ago, I was a Zen Master who lived on this mountain. One of my disciples asked me, 'Is an enlightened man subject to the law of cause and effect?' I answered that he is not, and have been reborn as a fox for the past five hundred years. I am still a fox. Will you answer the question, and save me? Is an enlightened person subject to the law of cause and effect?"

"The enlightened person is one with the law of cause and effect," answered Hyakujo, at which the old man was enlightened. He asked the master to perform his funeral, and then disappeared. The master searched around and found the dead body of a fox, and, to the dismay of the monks, gave it a full monastic funeral.

This story has been used by many generations of Zen monks as a subject for meditation. Why should a person who gives the wrong answer to a question be condemned to rebirth as a fox? How can a right answer set such a person free? What is the sense in such a story anyway? As a later master commented:

> ▶ *Subject or not subject*
> *Both are grievous error.*

Clearly there is no right answer, and many students have been given blows for offering a logical answer. The "right" answer is clearly no answer at all, and any answer that we give in judgement about another person's karma also deserves blows.

The second story is more personal, and relates to a friend of mine who had a very hard life.

> ▶ *This friend became interested in Buddhism, and used to attend a meditation group under the guidance of a certain teacher. Some of the disciples told him that all his troubles were due to bad karma brought over from a previous life. He pondered this long and hard, but decided in the end that he could not accept it.*
>
> *From that moment, his life began to get better. He was left a small amount of money from an unexpected source, invested it wisely in a property, which he sold for a profit, and, while he was never rich, generated enough to live on. He met a lady with whom he struck up a warm relationship, and eventually they married. Most of all, he developed a calm acceptance of life that was very different from his previous feelings of resentment.*
>
> *Some years later, he met the teacher once again, and told him his story. The teacher smiled and said, "Now you know!"*

Such stories illustrate the complexity of a human life. Karma is clearly more than just leftovers from previous lives. If change is the law, and there is in reality no self to experience anything, then the most important aspect of karma probably occurs in this life. Karma is here and now. This is why the Buddha discouraged speculation into previous or future lives. Even regarding enlightened beings, he said it is sheer foolishness to speculate whether they will survive death or not.

Most of my readers will have been born in the twentieth century. In the light of karma, there is a reason for this. It is a time that provides us with problems and opportunities that could not have occurred a hundred or a thousand years ago, to say nothing of the time of the Buddha. The problems of the twenty-first century will also be different. The timeless teachings of the Buddha are helpful in pointing us towards the causes of these problems but the application of those teachings and the solutions will have to be found in the here and now.

Something that relates specifically to the time we are born is astrology. The popularity of astrology is very great, but the implications are not fully understood. Most writings on Buddhism imply that it is mere superstition, not to be taken seriously, and to be avoided at all costs. While the Buddha was clear that we should not become involved in slavish adherence to anything, astrology was widely practiced in his time, and he would have known of it. His own future was predicted by some similar means, when his parents were told that he would become a great king or a great sage.

In most Buddhist countries astrology, oracles and predictive sciences are well-known and practiced. The Tibetan tradition is supported by oracles and by oracular systems, and few major decisions are made without reference to them. Astrology is popular among lay Buddhists in Thailand, Burma and Sri Lanka. Indian and Chinese astrology have co-existed with Buddhism for many centuries.

It seems to me that the principle to apply in this case is the same as for anything else. Is it helpful? It is not helpful if it suspends reason or if, as a result of "the stars," we are less kind and compassionate towards those who may be going through difficulties in their lives. Shakespeare's dictum that the truth lies not in our stars but in ourselves is good Dharma. However, even if in reality we do not have a "self," most of us live our daily lives as if our personality was one. Therefore, so long as we maintain "Right Views," anything that helps us to understand that personality and avoid more suffering may be considered helpful. And if it is helpful, it is good.

All birth is birth into form, and this creates responsibilities. We do not live without responsibilities. Our relationship with the world and with all the other beings who inhabit it with us makes us in part responsible for them. We are accountable for our bodies and minds, particularly insofar as we realize that they are not our selves. We are fortunate in the fact that we hear the Dharma, but once we have heard it, we are answerable for what we do with it.

The story of the Buddha's "Great Renunciation" leads some people to reject responsibilities. They feel that they too are capable of great renunciation, and that the Dharma is telling them that they have a duty to follow in their Master's footsteps. This can be a form of spiritual pride. The Buddha was born as Shakyamuni in response to his karma, and we are born today in response to ours. Contemporary life in the West is very different from that in India at the time of the Buddha.

The monastic followers of the Buddha were able to be truly homeless; to wander in the forest, to meditate at the foot of trees and rely completely on the generosity of the lay people for their sustenance. In return, they preached the Dharma. In Buddhist countries today most monks live in monasteries, and the majority of Buddhists are lay people. The essence of Buddhism is "skillful means," and this includes the understanding that different worlds need different methods.

According to some traditions, the Buddha foretold that his immediate teaching would not survive more than five hundred years after his passing. The following thousand years would see teaching and practice that were partially corrupt. Then would come the age of Dharma-ending, which would require different practices to lead beings to enlightenment. This is the age we are living in now. Today, most of us need to be "in the world but not of it"; to be "home-less" in the midst of the world. Whether this is possible I do not know, but I believe it is worth the effort to try.

However, it is not all bad. It is true that we have killed more people in the last hundred years than in the whole of our previous history, and we have weapons that can kill millions more. We have a so-called civilization that is based increasingly on profit and power. It is also true that wherever there is a disaster anywhere in the world, millions of ordinary people dig into their pockets and give to help alleviate the suffering. Charities work with sick, suffering, disadvan-taged and refugee people, and we have the United Nations as a place where politicians can negotiate in an attempt to avoid war, however ineffective it may seem to be. There is a growing awareness of the interdependence of all aspects of life on earth, and people who care enough to give up all or part of their lives to help heal the damage caused by those who put profits before harmony.

> ▶ *All in all,*
> *I think the world's karma is improving,*
> *But then I wouldn't really know.*
> *And nor would anyone else.*
> *We each have to make up our own minds,*
> *Or not.*
> *"Best not to speculate," the Buddha said,*
> *But it's up to you.*

But I Still Believe in God!

✦

Your home is Jesus or God.
Your home is Buddha or Buddhahood.

—THICH NHAT HANH, *GOING HOME*

One of the problems many Western people have with Buddhism is that they still believe in God. It may not be the God of the churches or the God of the priests and pastors, but recent surveys show that a consistently high percentage of the Western public still believe in God. This is another reason why people say, "I couldn't possibly be a Buddhist."

In conversations with a number of Western Buddhists about their beliefs and practices, I have been surprised by the number who admit that God is still important in their spiritual lives. I must confess to being pleased about this. Having been a Buddhist for nearly forty years and having come to Buddhism after rejecting Christianity, I am now clearer about the existence of God than I ever was as a member of the Christian Church. In the course of my journey I have discovered that the Dharma teaches us about the nature of God in ways that I could not have learned otherwise.

For many of us Western-born Buddhists with a basic Christian background, God will not go away, even if our upbringing was in an atheist or agnostic household. One aspect of this came to me in a conversation with a close friend who is neither a Buddhist nor a Christian. He asked me, "If you are a Buddhist, why is it that when you see something that upsets or shocks you, you still say, 'Oh God!'?" He was right. I must confess that I have not replaced my "Oh God!" with a Buddhist alternative, and, I have no desire to do so.

We are taught that Buddhism is a religion that has no place for God. The Buddha may not have actually rejected the existence of God, but he discouraged theological speculation to such an extent that it amounted to virtually the same thing. Many Buddhist teachers today take it even further, specifically denying the existence of God, and rejecting any mention of Him, Her or It.[11] Indeed, they seem to fear the very word, "God." It is as if acceptance of the word into their vocabulary will somehow dilute their Buddhism, or they will once again be drawn back into the Christianity that they have rejected.

There have been many famous Buddhists who are not bothered by the word, and have used it freely though in their own way. Such famous names as Bikkhu Buddhadasa, Ajahn Chah, D. T. Suzuki, Suzuki Roshi, Thich Nhat Hanh, the Dalai Lama, Lama Yeshe and Chogyam Trungpa have all included the word God in their writings. What do we mean by God, and what sort of God is it that Buddhists do not believe in?

Buddhists often base their unbelief on the teachings of theological fundamentalism. This is unfortunate, as this way of looking at God historically belongs to a time when the Western world was almost exclusively Christian, and to theology rather than mysticism. It makes no allowances for recent developments in scholarship, and excludes mystical, creation, post-modernist or feminist theologies.

For example, the idea of God as creator is taken from the first chapters of the Book of Genesis. Few Christians today accept this version of creation without reservation. Most agree that it is a myth that speaks only to those who are in tune with it. A re-reading of Genesis shows that the story itself is not consistent. There are, in fact, at least two creation stories. They are not definitive historical documents describing a once-and-for-all-time happening. In the Jewish mystical tradition, these stories are revealed as a mystical pathway to the understanding of creation as a continuous process. Continuous creation is change, the Buddha's teaching of anicca.

The idea of God as an all-powerful judge, who will send us to heaven or hell for all eternity, grew out of the political aspirations of the growing Christian Church. The threat of eternal hells is a great means to gain and retain a hold over the faithful. Buddhism has its hells too and while they are not eternal, they are frightening enough to have been used to keep the faithful in line. The concept of hell is not consistent with the original teachings of Gautama or Jesus, but was added to the scriptures later. Jesus' parables such as The Good Shepherd and The Prodigal Son confirm the true teaching, and they have their parallels in Buddhism. God is Unconditional Love, and it is impossible that anyone could ever be damned by such a God. If there is a hell, we bring it upon ourselves.

A side issue—but one that is important to bear in mind—is the divergence from the original teachings of Christianity, when the concept of rebirth was condemned as heresy. Rebirth was widely accepted by Christians up to the fourth century. Jesus himself is said to have referred to it in relation to John the Baptist when he stated that "John is the destined Elijah, if you will but accept it." If rebirth had not been widely accepted, there would have been no need for a council of senior bishops to condemn the teaching as heresy. If the Church's political and religious power over the people was to be enhanced by the fear of eternal damnation then rebirth had to go.

Some aspects of God definitely are found within Buddhist teaching. The Buddha spoke about the ". . . Unborn, Unmade, Unmanifest and Unbecome" without which there could be no escape from the born, made, manifest and become. Some Buddhist commentators say that this refers to the state of Nirvana and not to anything that could be confused with God, but remember that we do not know what Nirvana is. Maybe Nirvana is God. Bankei Zenji was clear that it referred to our own Buddha Mind or, as Christian mystics might say, God within us.

God is revealed within Christianity as Love. Many Buddhists concentrate on the Wisdom aspect of Buddhism but in my experience Buddhism is primarily about Love and Compassion. One of my teachers often told us to "Remember that Compassion is not just something you feel; it is the Buddha." In the Christian New Testament we are told that God is Love, and it would be a rare Buddhist who denied that Love exists. Buddhists all over the world spend some time each day in metta meditation, sending out thoughts of loving-kindness to the whole of this suffering world. Metta is something real, it is Love, and Love is God; Love is not something that God has or gives, but the very nature of Its being, which embraces all.

There is a story of a French Catholic priest whose duties included ministering to the dying.

▶ *Father Pascal was very happy in his work, but he suffered when he considered those who died outside the Church or who were very sinful. He thought they were destined for hell.*

One day, while he was at prayer, he had a mystical revelation of the Love of God. In a flash, he came to know that this was unconditional, for all creation, and that nothing and no one was excluded.

More than this, he knew that God is Love, and that Love is God.

This experience completely changed his life, and from then on he ministered joyfully to all who were dying, regardless of their religion or lifestyle, for now he knew that God was Love, and that Love rejected no one.

Similarly, Shinran Shonin's saying that "... if a good person goes to the Pure Land, how much more an evil person" embraces everyone. When I heard this, I understood the real meaning of Jesus' words that he had come to save sinners and not the righteous. It helped me to discover this aspect of the Divine within Buddhism and rediscover it in Christianity.

A similar argument applies to God seen as Life or as Light. In the Japanese Pure Land Traditions, Amida Buddha is the Buddha of Infinite Light and Eternal Life. This Light and Life permeate everywhere, leaving no room for the darkness of self. Whether from Buddha or God, *Infinite* Light leaves no room for a separate self, and so the teaching of *anatta* is true. Mystical writers from the Christian tradition talk about a similar Light, and tell us that God is most easily found through the letting go of self. This is the very essence of Buddhist thought and practice. When eventually we become enlightened, I wonder what language we will use? I doubt if we will care whether people call the Infinite "Buddha," "Mind," "Self" or "God."

We are also told that God may be found in the "Here and Now." This is mindfulness in Buddhist terms. God is also in the total acceptance of the inability of our minds to grasp the Infinite and Eternal, that is, in truthfully and honestly saying, "I don't know!" Many contemporary Christian mystics have been influenced by the *Tao Teh Ching*, finding in it one of the highest aspects of God. Buddhist sages in Japanese and Chinese traditions were also happy to use the term "Tao" in their teachings for both the Way and the Goal.

The Buddha emphasized that it is unskillful to speculate on the nature and powers of the Divine, which are essentially beyond our ability to grasp. Speculation distracts us from the goal of Nirvana. Even in the Hindu tradition, which was the Buddha's own, it is meditation—through which we come to *know* God—that is encouraged by the sages, rather than theology, where we seek to know *about* God.

Within Buddhism we find many personal aspects of God. They even have worlds of their own. Some are Hindu gods that would have been familiar to the Buddha, while others—such as some of the Chinese deities—belong to traditions that have intermingled with Buddhism. All are seen as still being subject to change and without a fixed separate self. Many have come to be regarded as guardians of the Dharma, while others co-exist within Buddhism and other faith traditions. A good example is Avalokiteshvara who, as Kwan Yin, is seen as a Bodhisattva within Buddhism, a manifestation of the Infinite Tao within Taoism, and a goddess within popular Chinese spirituality.

I have come to the conclusion that Western Buddhism needs to find a place for God, and that doing so does not necessarily mean rejecting any part of the Buddha's teaching. In fact, it may lead to a clearer understanding of some aspects of the Dharma. Rejecting Christianity (or any other religion) is not necessary for a Buddhist. In fact, Buddhism has a history of embracing existing religions and cultures, and the insights of the world's mystics embrace infinite possibilities.

Acquired knowledge of theology or buddhology does not mean that we are any further forward on the road to the Kingdom of Heaven or Nirvana. When I am told that the Unborn, or Love, or Life or Light is not the same as God, or that Nirvana or Sukhavati differs from the Kingdom of Heaven, I wonder what authority the speakers have. I find it helpful to challenge them—and myself—in the manner of the old Zen masters.

> ▶ *If there is anyone here who has achieved the Ultimate Goal,*
> *Through practices of both the Buddhist and Christian ways,*
> *Then I will listen to what they have to say.*
> *If there are such people here,*
> *Then I say, "Speak!"*

If there are not,
Then let us follow the example of the Buddha,
And keep quiet.
In the meantime,
Only accept those things which
Help us to see truth face to face.[12]

For me—and for many other Western Buddhists—this includes God.

Buddhism and Prayer

◆

In whatever direction you pray,
Pray according to your own beliefs.
I will be there in front of you,
And grant your requests.
Therefore, pray earnestly and with firm faith.

—MILAREPA

*A*nother of the great misconceptions about Buddhism is that Buddhists do not pray. Go into Buddhist temples anywhere in the world, and you will find Buddhists at prayer. The Buddha may not be a God, and neither may the great Bodhisattvas, but ordinary Buddhists the world over pray to them for spiritual and material blessings.

If you go into the main hall of most Buddhist temples, you will probably find devotees offering incense with joined palms, or bowing to the Buddha. They may be asking for something, but their practice is a prayer of worship and not of supplication. Ask any teacher of prayer within Christianity, Judaism or Islam, and they will tell you that worship is probably one of the highest forms of prayer. One of the best examples is the Islamic prayer that is offered five times a day, and is one of the practices that makes one a Muslim. This prayer is worship of Allah, and not a request for personal benefits.

When I was a young Catholic, we were taught that prayer is the lifting up of the mind and heart to God. This was written in the Catechism of that time, which Catholic children had to memorize, and I still remember it as one of the best definitions of prayer. This lifting up of the mind and heart to the highest that we can envisage is very much what ordinary Buddhists do in worshipping the Buddha.

If you go into one of the side chapels of a temple, you might find there an image of one of the forms of Avalokiteshvara. Because she is the manifestation of the Buddha's Compassion in the world, devotees have no hesitation is asking her for material things in a way that they might not do with the Buddha. They know the range of her compassion, and that for her there are no great or small requests. Her work is the removal of suffering, although this is what we might call a long-term project. More immediately, she does not feel offended if people ask for short-term help and for boons such as children, homes, sustenance and even money, provided their motives are right.

Prayers are also a part of many Buddhist liturgies. In the Tibetan and Chinese traditions, prayers are regularly offered as a part of the daily services, as well as for the long life of lamas and teachers. In other prayers the Buddhas are implored to visit the sacred space where the rite is being performed. Ceremonies are performed with the aim of healing, or of bringing certain benefits to the community or to the world. Prayers for peace are an integral part of many Buddhist practices. These liturgies are not just words, but deep spiritual practices. Prayer and meditation blend as supplication that may also include visualization of the deities and Buddhas, with the practitioner and the being visualized ultimately becoming blended in formless Mind.

In view of the fact that they do not have a conception of God as other religions do, it is quite reasonable to ask, "To whom are Buddhists praying?" They may pray to various Buddhas and Bodhisattvas, or may voice the prayer as their own wish or intention. An example of this is the practice of metta meditation, where thoughts of loving kindness are said to have a power of their own when backed by the intention of the meditator.

The question of this meditation as prayer is a controversial one. I remember having correspondence with a Theravadin monk in a national magazine devoted to spiritual healing. This monk had written to say that his tradition of Buddhism did not believe in prayer. I replied, asking him what he thought was happening when he practiced metta. Did he believe that the practice of wishing others well actually had an effect on them, or was it just for the benefit of the meditator? Several letters were exchanged through the columns of the magazine, but I do not think he ever answered the question. Yet many Buddhists practice this meditation daily for those who are sick, and are certain that it has good effects.

This is only one of the areas where prayer and meditation become one. In "The Koans of Life" we saw how one Buddhist became aware of what might reasonably be called approaches to prayer in and through his own experience. In particular, there is the "Zen word" and "finding the soul of things." In this poem, W. J. Gabb sums up the Zen approach of the highest form of prayer, moving instantly and easily from the infinite to the mundane, from the sublime to the ridiculous. Anyone who has lost—or found—themselves walking by the sea will instantly identify with these thoughts.

> ▶ *I walked upon an empty beach,*
> *Where there was none to see.*
> *I ran, and laughed, and danced, and called*
> *And no one answered me.*
> *I revelled in the driving rain,*
> *With none to say me nay,*
> *Companioned only by the clouds*
> *That sped the dying day.*

And then it came to me to pray.
I prayed to nobody.
I asked for nothing, wished for naught,
I simply sought to be.
To BE, not fettered by the flesh,
But free to do and dare,
Intangible, ineffable,
A word, a breath, a prayer.

What happened? Nothing happened
For a million years or so.
I guess I walked and talked with God
But then … I wouldn't know.
My wife said, "Billie, why so late,
We've nearly finished tea?"
I told her, "Sorry, darling,
I've been strolling by the sea."

Here, prayer and meditation are combined. There is no separation, no duality and no concern as to what is happening at any moment. One does not have to be a Buddhist to experience this sort of mystical prayer. The archives of the Religious Experience Research Centre are filled with accounts of people who have had similar experiences, both within and outside the context of religion. Yet to consciously "pray to nobody," asking for nothing and simply seeking to be is difficult, because it is venturing into the realm of the Great Unknown.

▶ *A man was running away from a hungry lion.*
Suddenly he found himself on the edge of a great cliff.
While the lion crouched and snarled, he prayed, "Is there anyone there? Please help me."
With infinite sweetness, a voice answered out of nowhere, "Jump over the cliff, and you will be caught in the Everlasting Arms."
The man paused just a moment, and then cast his eyes up to heaven and said, "Is there anyone else there?"

We can all sympathize.

In Chinese and Japanese the same word is used for both mind and body. It is my experience that in praying for others mind and heart, prayer and meditation blend. Some years ago I wrote a booklet on the prayer of "Don't Know!"[13] This concept is found with Christian writings like *The Cloud of Unknowing*, but I had first found it within Zen Buddhism. The contemporary Korean master, Seung Sahn, has said that "Don't know mind is next to enlightened mind." Some of my most profound prayer experiences have come about when I have started by honestly admitting that I do not know how to pray for something. Being honest about this quickly brings the mind to stillness, and opens it to receive intuitive guidance. It is becoming like a little child, as Jesus taught, or the "Beginner's Mind" of the Zen Master Suzuki Roshi.

Even within the most iconoclastic aspects of Zen Buddhism one finds prayer. Hakuin Zenji, a Zen master who completely reformed Zen Buddhism with his insistence on the koan tradition, used to recognize that there were those of his disciples for whom prayer was essential. Towards the end of his life he took an increasing interest in the world outside the monastery, and in the lives and practices of his lay disciples. In a letter dated 1794 to Lord Nabeshima, he talks about the great merits to be gained by the recitation of a particular invocation to Kannon (Kwan Yin), known as the Ten Phrase Life Prolonging Kannon Sutra. One is that the person who recites it regularly will be completely free from disease, and will have their life prolonged.

▶ *There was a man in China called Kao-huang who was sentenced to be executed. He was an ardent devotee of Kwan Yin.*

On the night before his execution he was meditating on Kwan Yin when the Bodhisattva appeared to him. He was told that if he could recite the Sutra a thousand times in the night his life would be saved. Though he thought it would be impossible, he decided to try.

The next morning when he was due to be beheaded the sword snapped, and so did all the others that were tried. The executioner

demanded to know what was happening, whereupon he was told the
story, and Kao-huang's life was spared.

The Sutra can be chanted in any language, though it does not actually make literal sense when translated into English. However, the
following was given to me by a devotee when I published an article
about it in *Pure Land Notes,* and I think it goes a good way towards
expressing the essence in English.

▶ *Kwan Shih Yin!*
We are one with Buddha.
In him, the cause,
In him, the refuge.
Buddha-Dharma-Sangha is our refuge!

Our true nature is not-self.
Awareness comes from Mind,
And is not separate from Mind.
In the morning, Kwan Shih Yin with awareness!
In the evening, Kwan Shih Yin with awareness!

He claimed to use it regularly with surprising results, including
visions of the Bodhisattva and healing of a condition that had trou-
bled him for many years. In Western terms this would be the practice of prayer for, as we have seen, prayer and meditation are really
not that far apart.

The denial of prayer within Buddhism is another example of
the doctrinaire approach that has come to us by taking only the so-
called highest aspects of the teaching. I hope I have said enough to
allow Buddhists who wish to pray to do so without any qualms, and
to allow people of other faiths interested in Buddhism to feel that
their prayer life is unaffected. Buddhism in the West will be richer if
the practice of prayer becomes a part of it as it is in the rest of the
Buddhist world.

Buddhism and Christianity

◆

Buddha equals Christ
Equals Buddha
Equals Christ.

—Ling Chao

Because of my links with both Buddhism and Christianity I have been involved for many years in helping people in the reconciliation of ideas, as well as leading retreats and study courses for those interested in both faiths. My own life as a Buddhist has been a search for ways of reconciling my Christian background with my Buddhist faith. In this I have been helped by my studies with Rev. Jack Austin, my association with the Religious Society of Friends (Quakers) and the Christian–Buddhist Dialogue group of which I have been a member since it started ten years ago.

Even after discovering Buddhism, for many years I carried a great resentment towards the Roman Catholic Church that I had been born and brought up in. This led to problems with my mother who was an ardent Catholic, and lived at some distance from us. I did not take on board the significance of the Buddha's teaching that hatred is never conquered by hatred, only by love, and that all religious faiths should be respected. I maintained that attitude for a number of years, until I met the Rev. Jack Austin. Jack was a Buddhist priest, and had long before reconciled his Christian background with his Buddhism. He was also a member of the Cathedral Choristers Association, and regularly took his annual retreat in a Catholic monastery dressed in his Buddhist robes, where he was fully accepted as a member of the community. Jack told me, "If you hate the Roman Catholic Church, or even Christianity, you are as bound by it as if you love it." These words were like a lightning bolt, and set me free from hatred and resentment. I am eternally grateful for his wise words.

Several years after becoming a Buddhist I encountered the Quakers. When our local Buddhist group folded, I missed the weekly meditation. I was advised by someone to go to the local Quaker meeting, which he thought was another form of meditation. In some ways it is, but anyone may speak in the silence at any time they feel inspired. It was some weeks before this happened, and I realized that Quaker Meeting for Worship (as they call it) was not quite the same as Buddhist meditation. I decided that if I were to continue, I had to know more.

The Quakers include a variety of beliefs, from Universal to Christocentric, and it was the former that, many years later, led to my being persuaded to apply for membership. Part of the membership procedure is being visited by two Friends to see if you are suitable. I had made no secret of my Buddhism, and I was not surprised to be asked if I was a Christian. "What do you mean by a Christian?" I asked. "All right," they said, "What do you think of Jesus?" I replied that I thought his life and teaching was something that I might try to live up to for my next ten lifetimes, an answer I still give. To my surprise, this was accepted, and I became a Quaker.

This is not the place to go into Quaker beliefs, but an important one is that they believe God is in each person in the form of what they call "The Inward Light." This was close enough to the Unborn

Buddha Mind to allow me to feel at home and, in spite of a few theological differences with some Friends, I have continued to do so.
My journey with Friends led me to work for their central organization for eighteen years, and to be asked to write a book on Quaker
spirituality called *Listening to the Light*, which has been well received
both in the Society of Friends and elsewhere.

Whether we own it or not, most of us are deeply influenced
by Christianity. With so many years of history, it could not be otherwise. We are influenced by it even if we consciously reject it. I believe
that it is important for Western Buddhists to come to terms with the
Christian influences in their lives, and with those parts of Christianity
that they have either accepted or rejected. My personal experience of
the conflict that can be caused if the two are not reconciled has led
me to explore ways in which a reconciliation can be facilitated.

There is increasing dialogue and interaction between Buddhism
and Christianity. Every year there are a number of Buddhist/Christian
retreats, and there are many other ways in which Buddhism and
Christianity are influencing each other. I know of many Christians,
even Christian priests and nuns, who practice Buddhist meditation.
I also know of many Buddhists who have been inspired by Christians
to apply their Buddhist teachings towards the alleviation of the ills
of society and the world. Books by prominent Buddhists such as His
Holiness The Dalai Lama, and the Venerable Thich Nhat Hanh look
closely at the teachings of Buddha and Jesus, and they find enough
similarities to encourage deep dialogue.

For the last ten years I have been a member of a Buddhist–
Christian Dialogue Group that meets by invitation twice a year. Up
to twenty Christians and a similar number of Buddhists from varying traditions come together and share meditation, talks, dialogue
and a bring-and-share lunch. In some ways the lunch is most important, as it gives space to discuss personal matters that cannot be shared
in open meeting. Many deep and warm friendships have been made,

and many difficult matters discussed. The purpose of the group is not to come to any conclusions, but to support each member in their life and work.

Many Buddhists recognize the Dharma in Christian life and thought, particularly in the teachings of Jesus. As well as those mentioned above, Zen masters, including some of my own teachers, have also recognized this. Sanuki used to take us into Christian churches to meditate. He had evolved his own "Christian Koan"; "How can it be that Jesus and the Virgin Mary are both manifestations of Kannon Bodhisattva?" Roshi Furukawa shared a retreat center in the hills of southern Japan with a Catholic priest and two nuns. Roshi and his family would regularly meet with the Catholics to share prayer, meditation and chanting.

Teachers of many schools of Buddhism knew of the Bible and the teachings of Jesus. The following stories from two different Buddhist traditions illustrate this timeless acceptance of the Dharma, wherever it is to be found.

▶ *One of Gasan's students asked him, "Have you ever read the Christian Bible?"*

"No," said the Master, "Read it to me."

The student opened the Bible and read from the Gospel of St. Matthew.

"Why be anxious about clothing? Consider the lilies of the field, how they grow. They do not toil, neither do they spin, and yet I say unto you that even Solomon in all his glory was not arrayed like one of these. . . . Take therefore no thought for tomorrow, for tomorrow will look after itself."

Gasan listened with rapt attention. "Whoever said those words was an enlightened man," he commented.

The student continued: "Ask and you shall receive; seek and you will find; knock and the door will be opened. For everyone who asks, receives, they who seek, find, and they who knock will find the door opened."

"Whoever said that is not far from Buddhahood," said Gasan.

When Tibetan lamas first came into contact with Christianity, there was for some an instant recognition. This story of a Portuguese priest who came to Tibet some time in the eighteenth century was told to me by a Tibetan lama who had heard it from his own teacher. He loved the Jesus of the Gospels, and there was a small crucifix on the shrine in the house in which he lived. When I asked him the meaning of this he told me the story. I do not remember the actual names of the individuals concerned in this story, so I have invented them. Otherwise the story is as I was told it.

> ❱ *When Father Paulo arrived in Lhasa, he was welcomed by senior Buddhist monks. "I have come to teach your people about Jesus, who was the Son of God," he said. "May I have a space where I can celebrate his rites?"*
>
> *The monks agreed to provide him with a room and an altar, but asked that a representative could attend the mass, in order to ensure that there was nothing that would be offensive to their Buddhist ideals. The priest agreed.*
>
> *An elderly and much respected lama of the Nyingma or old school, Shentong Rinpoche, was deputed to assist the priest, in the belief that he might have a greater understanding of unorthodox rites. He was a good listener, and soon made friends with the priest.*
>
> *"What did this Jesus do?" Shentong asked.*
>
> *"He came to earth from his home in heaven to save us from our sins by dying a cruel death on the cross," replied the priest.*
>
> *"Oh!" said the lama, "I understand. He was a Great Bodhisattva."*
>
> *The priest produced a crucifix, and set it on the altar. He then left the room to change his clothes in order to celebrate the mass.*
>
> *When he returned, he found the old monk performing full-length prostrations before the crucifix, while reciting "Om Mani Padme Hum," the mantra of Chenrezig, the Bodhisattva of Compassion.*

I was told that the priest gave his crucifix to the lama when he left Tibet. The lama kept it on his shrine, and honored it each day with full Buddhist rites, and this was passed down from teacher to pupil.

The lama who told me this story was a direct spiritual descendant of Lama Shentong.

Once I had solved my problems with the Catholic Church, I discovered that not only did Buddhism have much to teach me about the teachings of Jesus, but that the reverse was also true. There are three Christian books which, though they talk about God rather than Buddha, have been a great inspiration to me. In the first one, it is just the title that inspires me: *Your God Is Too Small* by J. B. Phillips. I read the book, but it was not for me. However, the title tells me that any thought that I may have about God is certainly not the whole truth, and may not even approach truth at all. It gives me an inkling as to why the Buddha refused to talk about God. If I say anything, then my God is too small. The same truth is found in the *Tao Teh Ching*, where we are told, "The Tao that can be spoken of is not the Eternal Tao."

The second book is Brother Lawrence's *Practice of the Presence of God*. This was a book that Sanuki knew and loved, and carried with him in his journeys around the world. I will not easily forget my surprise at having a former Zen monk recommending a book by a Catholic lay brother. This work can be translated into Buddhist terms, and provides the basis of a practice that many Buddhists do without being aware of it. If we can accept that God is in the Here and Now, then it is clear that the practice of the Presence of God is the same as mindfulness and insight. It is not just the practice of sitting that leads to enlightenment, but the daily moment-by-moment practice.

The third book is another little spiritual classic, *The Way of a Pilgrim*. The pilgrim is given the Jesus prayer to recite many hundreds of times each day, just as Pure Land Buddhists are given the Nembutsu. The part that was really helpful to me is where he describes the prayer as descending from the head to the heart. This helped me to understand what Shinran Shonin calls "Shinjin" (literally, "a true heart") in a new way.

I have become convinced of the importance of the relationship of Buddhists and Christians. I feel very strongly that each has much to give the other, and that they are to a great extent complementary. I think it was Arnold Toynbee who said that when we look back we will see that the history of the world was influenced to a great extent by the relationship between Buddhism and Christianity in the twentieth century. I believe this may be even more true in the twenty-first.

The following meditation can be done by either Buddhists or Christians (just substitute the name "Christ" for the name "Buddha").

> ▶ *Think for a moment of all the meanings of "Buddha" given in this book.*
> *Add to this all that the word "Buddha" means to you.*
> *Then think of what it means to the millions of Buddhists throughout the world.*
> *Think of the wonder of the living man—who was more than just a man.*
> *Then call to mind all the universal dimensions of Buddhahood.*
> *The various manifestations of Shakyamuni Buddha.*
> *Think of the wonder of Buddha-Nature in all beings,*
> *and the infinite variety this represents*
> *In human beings*
> *In animals*
> *In the vegetable kingdom*
> *In the very earth Itself!*
> *All this is "Buddha"*
> *And so much more,*
> *More than we can ever embrace with our minds.*
>
> *If "Buddha" is all this and so much more for Buddhists, then so must "Christ" be for Christians.*
> *So how can either reject what is just another aspect of the Great Mystery?*

I once dreamt that the Buddha and Christ met, and they embraced, laughed and even cried together before sharing a deep silence. They did not discuss Buddhism or Christianity. I wonder why?

Buddhism F.O.C. (Free of Charge)

✦

*The Buddha-dharma
does not reside
In fame and profit-making.*

—ZUIKEN

everal years ago, the Buddhist magazine *Tricycle* featured a short article entitled "Buddhism on No Dollars a Day," which I found most inspiring. I had been worried by the discrepancy between the teaching I had received that no charge should be made for teaching the Dharma, and the apparent exploitation of Dharma teaching that was going on in some places. Many of the Buddhist publications that I received were full of advertisements offering talks, meditation weekends, seminars, retreats and even "enlightenment intensives," whatever they might be. Most of them quoted fees, many of which were far beyond my ability to afford, even had I wanted to go on them.

Shortly after reading the article, which seemed to pass unnoticed by most of the other Buddhists that I knew, I received a letter from a friend in which he commented on the general Western Buddhist scene. He had not read the article but raised similar points in his letter:

▶ *Sometimes I wonder what is going on here, and what kind of people are taking up Buddhism. I know that it has become popular due to various Hollywood and similar types, but it seems that to follow some of the teachers, you have to be a millionaire or something similar. I will not be surprised if we soon see Buddhist teachers listed among the richest people in the U.S.*

This does not bother me too much, as most of my practice is at home, but I do feel kind of nervous to confess that I am a Buddhist in case people think that I'm rich.

I understand Buddhist teachers have to live, and accept that they may have to teach full-time, and not only in addition to another job. To teach meditation effectively takes a lot of time and effort, a great deal of preparation, and quite a lot of physical and mental energy. I do not feel that the future of Buddhism in the West lies solely within the monastic tradition, though even within that tradition by no means all adhere to the spirit of "the homeless life" with its refusal to handle money. I do feel that "right livelihood" has a definite place in the teaching of the Dharma. The big question is one of balance.

Many Buddhist meetings and weekends have the tradition of asking for a donation, and suggesting what that donation might be. This is fine, provided the principle is adhered to that no one should be denied the teaching for lack of funds. This is the basic principle that governed the Buddha's life and teaching, and I feel that it should have a pride of place in all Dharma dealings.

I also appreciate that there is a need for centers. I do get a bit worried when I see repeated appeals for funds to maintain or set up centers, with the implication that there could be no Buddhism without them. Buddhism does not depend on having centers. The most important thing is daily practice, and this can be done in the home, or in any suitable place outside such as under a tree, weather permitting.

What do we *need* to practice Buddhism? Nothing at all, absolutely nothing! Special places, shrines, Buddha images, teachers, other people, scriptures or commentaries can be helpful, but are not essential. We might actually need some of these things to practice Buddhism, but it should be clear by now that we do not need any of them for the practice of the Dharma.

Buddhism is the religion that has grown out of the Buddha-Dharma. It has evolved out of the teaching of the Buddha. As it is essentially something that changes all the time, it must take its shape out of the experience of those who practice it. The Buddha told his followers that the best place to meditate would be against the trunk of a tree. The Buddha himself achieved his nirvana under a tree, which forever became known as the *Bo* (enlightenment) tree, and trees have had a special place in Buddhist thought ever since.

These first followers of the Buddha-Dharma did not have any form of shrine. In fact, the Buddha-Dharma was a reaction against the power of the temples and their priests, just as the Gospel was in Jesus' time. Early symbols of the Buddha were not the well-known Buddha image, but a footprint indicating one of the titles of the Buddha, *Tathagata*, the one who has "thus gone"; or the eight-spoked chakra wheel standing for the eightfold path. Many modern Zen teachers have used informal shrines that do not contain a Buddha image. Sanuki used to have a scroll with the calligraphy for "Remember!" on it, together with a single flower ("I like fresh flowers," he used to say, "but I don't pick more than I can help") and a stick of incense. Other teachers have used unusually shaped stones or pieces of driftwood, saying that the Buddha-Nature in them is as real as in an image, maybe more so as the image restricts the Buddha to a particular form.

Though a teacher is a vital part of some schools of Buddhism (for example, in some Zen and Tibetan traditions) others say that we do not need a human teacher. For them, the Buddha is still our teacher. The Buddha said that after he died, the Dharma would be our teacher, but I think that Buddha and Dharma are One. As W. J. Gabb said, the real teacher is life.

This is also true for me, though I give grateful thanks for all my teachers, human and otherwise. I have acknowledged the main human ones at the beginning of the book, but there are many others who have an impact on my life in ways of which I am often not fully aware. Occasionally, I may be walking down a road, feeling somewhat low, and I will pass somebody who has an immediate effect of raising my spirits. This happened to me again yesterday in Oxford. I do not know why. It was not that they had a particularly striking face, or that they seemed unusual in any way, but as I walked past, I felt my mind clear, and my body walking taller. I wish I had the courage to approach such a person, but maybe I am not meant to.

I have learned a lot from cats and dogs, and also from trees.

▶ *Cats have taught me to relax, to be constantly aware.*
They embody relaxation,
yet are able to be instantly alert if the need arises.
I often think of this when I am waking up in the morning,
my eyes and my being still full of sleep.
They have shown me ways of acceptance; not to try to do things that are
beyond me.
They have also shown me how to play,
and taught me that play is an important part of life.

Dogs are similar in many ways,
They too can relax and yet be instantly alert.
They have a robustness and an overt loyalty that is a part of their being.
They show me how to manifest exuberant joy,
and how to be pleased by little things
and kind words.

Trees bring me calm, peace and patience.
They also bring energy.

If you sit and meditate with your back to a large tree,
you will feel it supporting you;
you will feel its energy recharging you.
You will feel your mind becoming still,
as if you come to share the mind of the tree.
You can even ask questions,
and it is as if the tree, from its greater age and wisdom,
is able to answer you.
Or, maybe, it is the tree's role to be a channel for the Buddha-mind
And your Buddha-mind is manifest through the tree.

The fellowship or community of the Sangha is one of the three Jewels of Buddhism and for many people is an essential part of practicing the Dharma. But Sangha in reality is spiritual friendship. Ananda, the Buddha's attendant, went to the Buddha and said that he had come to see that spiritual friendship was half of the spiritual life. "Say not so, Ananda," said the Buddha. "Spiritual Friendship is the whole of the spiritual life." However, if you feel that spiritual friendship can only occur with people who call themselves "Buddhists," then you are missing out on a great deal. I have been fortunate to have spiritual friends from all religions and none. Each of us can learn from others, and it may be that other people have a natural affinity for the Dharma in relationship to life's problems, without ever labelling themselves.

It is possible to be a part of a Buddhist Sangha without having a particular place for meetings. Contact can be made through correspondence, the telephone and occasional meetings, while the possibilities offered by the internet and e-mail are only just being explored. Sometimes we have to fulfill our karma in relation to friends or family who are not Buddhist, or may even be hostile to Buddhism. This may be necessary for a while but all things change, and it often causes far less karmic debris if we wait for change to happen naturally. Our inner life is always our own, and no one can control it unless we let them.

So, what do we need to practice the Dharma? Absolutely nothing! In fact, ABSOLUTELY NO-THING! The Dharma is beyond duality, beyond having and not having. It is beyond all the paraphernalia of Buddhism or any religion, yet can be found in them all. In the words of Seng T'san, the third Patriarch of Zen:

> ▶ *There is no difficulty about the Great Way*
> *Simply avoid choosing!*
> *When there is neither love not hate*
> *It is there in all clearness.*
> *Deviate by even the thickness of a hair,*
> *And there is a deep gulf between heaven and earth.*

No difficulty? Simple? Who is he kidding? However, one thing is clear. The Great Way is not a toll road, and it need not cost you anything to walk it.

Walk on!

The Way Ahead

Let's Walk Together

✦

*T*he previous chapter closed with an invitation to "Walk On!" "But," you may ask, "in which direction do I go? This Dharma that you have presented is something that rings bells with me, but I do not know how to proceed. The Dharma may be One, but Buddhism offers many alternatives. How do I proceed?"

This is perfectly true. The 2000 edition of the *Buddhist Directory*, which lists Buddhist groups throughout the United Kingdom, contains 372 entries, and the index of groups by tradition lists 31 different traditions. Some of these are further fragmented by being under the direction of different teachers. There are also some groups who did not wish to be included and this was respected. There are many opportunities for study and practice that come under the general heading of "Buddhism."

I can only answer your question by saying how it is for me. In writing this book, I have presented Buddhism as it impacts upon my life. What I have tried to present is the Dharma, which is simple and straightforward, though able to be approached through many gateways. Buddhism is incredibly complex, and is presented in so many ways that I often wonder if it is the same religion that is being offered. There are Thai Buddhists, Tibetan Buddhists, Chinese and Japanese Buddhists, Eastern and Western Buddhists, lay Buddhists and monastic Buddhists, to name but a few.

I cannot limit myself to any of these. I only try to follow the Dharma, and if this makes me any kind of Buddhist it will have to be one who recognizes and accepts his roots in Western culture, religion and form. While I accept and am grateful for the influence and inspiration that comes from my friends and teachers in China, Japan, Tibet and Sri Lanka, the Dharma will only make sense if it relates to my life as it is. If you are attracted by one or more of the cultural aspects of Buddhism, by all means explore them. You may be fortunate to find good teachers who will also respect your own heritage.

As I see it, walking on entails three very important steps. The first is to know where you are starting from. The second is to know and accept your companions, and the third is to cease worrying about your goal. These are best considered in a contemplative frame of mind.

▶ *Where you are starting from is where you are now, physically,*
mentally, philosophically, religiously and culturally.
Look at the whole picture, and see why you may need to move
forward.
There is probably a feeling of dissatisfaction or incompleteness with what
you have.
However, it is not possible to move on until you have have accepted
things as they are.
Look at every aspect of your life and thought.
See how they shape your life, how they help and hinder you.
How they bring you joy and sorrow.
Accept them and give thanks for them, for you could not be you without
them.

Once you have looked at all this, as it is now, then you can survey your traveling companions.

◗ *Your first companion is all that you are, all that you have discovered in the above exercise.*

All this must come with you, to provide a platform from which what you will discover is able to relate to your life as it is.

Next are the teachings of the Buddha, in particular that Kalama Sutra, which allows you the freedom to accept only those things that are clearly helpful to you and to others.

Then there are the Signs of Being, the Four Noble Truths and the Eightfold Path.

Do they make sense to you?

Even if you cannot live up to them at all times, are they sufficiently helpful for you to try?

Next comes the Buddha himself.

A man who showed us how to become truly human.

And more than human.

Is his example inspiring, and his teaching (the Dharma) helpful?

Lastly, there is the Sangha.

These are the friends and teachers that you meet along the way, both physically and through the written word.

Do not rush this process. Rather let your Sangha unfold itself in its own time and way.

Be prepared to test teachers thoroughly before making any commitment.

And know that the companionship of spiritual friends is more important than their advice.

Above all, be true to yourself in all things.

Finally, there is the goal.

In the journey of the Dharma, the goal is Nirvana, but remember that even the Buddha was reluctant to define this.

So do not try.

You may know when you get there

But it may not be important to you then.

In one sense, it is the journey that is important,

And every step is vital.

So just resolve to make every step as compassionate as you can,

And that is enough.

I will say how it is for me right now. I am writing this at Christmas time, when I have celebrated with my Christian friends and neighbors the birth of one who is, for them, as important as the Buddha is for me. (And, incidentally, who remains as important for me as ever.) While I sit and write, I have some peaceful Christmas Gregorian chant playing on the music center. It could just as easily be Japanese *shakuhachi* (bamboo flute), but the chanting seems more appropriate to the time. There is no conflict in going with what feels right, unless I allow my mind to say, "This isn't right! You are a Buddhist. Why are you listening to Christian music?"

The track that is playing is the *Kyrie Eleison* (Lord have Mercy) and my thoughts are turned not only to the fact that we all need grace from beyond ourselves to help in our journey, but also to those who are homeless or alone at this time. Such thoughts of compassion are inspired by the music, and so they are a means of grace for me, which I would be foolish to reject on grounds of religious prejudice. Other times I might get suitable inspiration from Tibetan or Japanese Buddhist chanting, from modern or traditional jazz or from the music of the Incredible String Band or Quintessence.

What I have learned is that walking on from where we are does not necessarily mean changing our religion, or even adopting a formal religion at all. It does not mean becoming a Buddhist, though you can if you want to. The teaching of the Buddha is that the Dharma is a Way of Life. If we want to practice this within temple or church, society or sangha, it is up to us. There is no one way.

So, in the spirit of the *Kalama Sutra*, take what is helpful and use it. Do not worry about what you cannot accept. If I have put it in this book it is because I have found it helpful, but this does not mean that you will. However, it is always there if you want to come back to it.

Notes and References

✦

1. "Not lo here or lo there, but the Kingdom of Heaven is within you." *Gospel of St Luke*: 17:21.
2. Marco Pallis; *A Buddhist Spectrum* (see Bibliography).
3. A translation of Mumon's *The Gateless Gate* can be found in *Zen Flesh, Zen Bones* by Paul Reps and Nyogen Senzaki.
4. Translations of and commentary on the Pure Land scriptures will be found in Hisao Inagaki's *The Three Pure Land Sutras* (see Bibliography).
5. Much of the information in this chapter is taken from John Blofeld's book, which was later re-issued as *Bodhisattva of Compassion* (see Bibliography).
6. Walter C. Lanyon; *London Notes and Lectures*, L. N. Fowler, London, no date given, but probably early 1930s.
7. An English translation of this work is part of the book, *Tiger's Cave* by Trevor Leggett (see Bibliography).
8. *The Way of Compassion*, published by Cambridge Buddhist Association, Cambridge, MA, 1966.
9. The title of his book on mantras is called *Mantras: Sacred Words of Power* (see Bibliography).
10. *Foundations of Tibetan Mysticism* by Lama Govinda.

11. I do not mind which pronoun people use for God, and am happy with He, She or It. Buddhists might tend to prefer "It," but there are times when the personal pronoun is necessary.

12. The Cambodian Buddhist Master, Maha Ghosananda, uses this phrase in his rendering of the *Kalama Sutra* in his book, *Step by Step.* "Accept and live only according to what will enable you to see truth face to face."

13. *What Kind of God, What Kind of Healing* (see Bibliography).

Glossary

◆

This Glossary gives the meanings of words as used in this book. For further information consult a good Buddhist dictionary or dictionary of religion (see Bibliography).

Amitabha: the Buddha of Infinite Light.

Amitayus: the Buddha of Eternal Life; another name for Amitabha.

Amida: Japanese name for Amitabha/Amitayus.

Anatta: literally "not-self." The teaching that there is nothing that we can call a fixed self.

Anicca: change or impermanence.

Anjin: literally "a settled heart"; firm belief and trust [in the Buddha].

Arahat (Arhat) (Arahant): an enlightened being in the Theravadin tradition.

Avalokiteshvara: the Bodhisattva of Compassion. "The one who hears the cries of the World."

Bhaisajya Guru: the Medicine Buddha; the principle Buddha of healing.

Bikkhu: one who has been ordained, or undertaken the homeless life. Often translated as "monk."

Bodhisattva: one who has attained enlightenment, but forgoes the final stage in order to help suffering beings.

Buddha: a fully enlightened being; one who has achieved enlightenment though his own efforts.

Buddhology: the Buddhist equivalent of theology.

Ch'an: literally the Chinese term for the Sanskrit Dhyana, meditation; the Chinese term for the Zen school.

Chenrezig: the Tibetan male form of Avalokiteshvara.

Dharma: the law; the Way; the teaching of the Buddha.

Dukkha: the unsatisfactory nature of life; suffering in its widest sense.

F.O.C.: literally "free of charge"; the concept that we do not need anything to be a Buddhist.

Hinayana: literally "the lesser vehicle" as opposed to the Mahayana; it is now considered a pejorative term, and little used except in some scholarly works. The only remaining Hinayana tradition is the Theravada.

Ji: temple; times.

Ji-shu: Japanese "Times" school, founded by Ippen Shonin, so-called because they recited the Buddha's name at fixed times throughout the day.

Jodo: Japanese for the Pure or Happy Land of Amida Buddha.

Jodoshu: Japanese Pure Land School, founded by Honen Shonin.

Jodoshinshu: Japanese True Pure Land School founded by Shinran Shonin.

Kannon: Japanese form of Kwan Yin; can be either male or female.

Kwan Yin: Chinese female form of Avalokiteshvara.

Mahaprajnaparamita: the (usually female) manifestation of the Prajnaparamita.

Mahayana: the Greater Vehicle; the Buddhism of Tibet and the Far East.

Maitreya: the Buddha to come.

Mi Lo Fo: Chinese form of Maitreya; see Pu T'ai.

Nembutsu: a Japanese term that literally means remembrance of the Buddha, but these days mostly refers to the chanting of the name of Amida Buddha.

Nirvana: the goal of Buddhism; however, the Buddha refused to talk about it and so do others who are supposed to have achieved it.

Nyingma: the oldest Tibetan School of Buddhism, otherwise known as the Red-hats.

Parinirvana: the death and final nirvana of a Buddha.

Prajnaparamita: literally the Wisdom Gone Beyond; the teaching that all is essentially emptiness or void.

Pu T'ai: a tenth-century Chinese Ch'an monk who was supposed to be an incarnation of Maitreya.

Pure Land: the Buddha world created by Amida, where there are no obstacles to our enlightenment.

Quakers: The Religious Society of Friends, founded in the seventeenth century and still going strong.

Roshi: literally Old Boy; a title of respect given to Japanese Zen sages.

Samadhi: a deep state of meditation.

Samma: right, perfect, best.

Shakyamuni: "the sage of the Shakyas" (the Buddha's family or clan).

Shin: "true" and also "heart or mind."

Shinjin: literally a true heart; the state of enlightenment where a practitioner of the Pure Land traditions knows their oneness with Amida Buddha.

Skandhas: literally heaps or aggregates; the constituents of a living being.

Sukhavati: Sanskrit for the Pure or Happy land.

Sunyata: void; emptiness.

Sutra: a teaching of the Buddha.

Sutta: the Pali form of Sutra.

Tao: literally the Way; the Infinite; the Eternal according to Taoism and adopted by Chinese Buddhism.

Tara: the Tibetan female Bodhisattva of Compassion, said to be born of a tear shed by Avalokiteshvara for the suffering of the world; vowed always to manifest in a female form.

Tathagata: "the one who has thus come" (or "gone"); one of the titles of the Buddha.

Theravada: the Buddhism of Thailand, Burma, Sri Lanka and Cambodia, based on the Pali scriptures.

Tendai: eclectic Japanese school of Buddhism, based on the Lotus Sutra; their practice includes meditation, chanting and Nembutsu.

Unborn: the Buddha said that there was an Unborn, and that because of it there was a way out of the born (suffering). Nobody really knows what he meant. Some say it is Nirvana, others Buddha Nature, and some think it was his one reference to God.

Zen: literarily, meditation. Japanese Buddhist school, which is iconoclastic and emphasizes meditation; Zen can also be a synonym for Life itself.

Bibliography
◆

Books Mentioned in the Text

Blofeld, John, *Compassion Yoga: The Mystical Cult of Kuan Yin.* London: Allen & Unwin, 1977 (later re-issued in paperback as *Bodhisattva of Compassion: The Mystical Tradition of Kuan Yin.* Boston: Shambhala Publications, 1988).

————, *Mantras: Sacred Words of Power.* London: Allen & Unwin, 1977.

Blyth, R. H., *Zen and Zen Classics* (5 volumes). Tokyo: Hokuseido Press, 1960–62.

————, *Zen in English Literature and Oriental Classics.* Tokyo: Hokuseido Press, 1942.

Buddhist Texts. Sri Lanka: Wheel Publishers.

Gabb, W. J., *The Goose Is Out.* London: The Buddhist Society, 1956.

Ghosananda, Maha, *Step by Step.* Berkeley: Parallax Press, 1991.

Haskel, Peter, trans., and Yoshito Hakeda, ed., *Bankei Zen.* New York: Grove Press, 1989.

Inagaki, Hisao, *The Three Pure Land Sutras.* Kyoto: Nagata Bunshodo, 1994.

Leggett, Trevor, *Tiger's Cave*. London: Rider Books, 1964.

Pallis, Marco, *A Buddhist Spectrum*. London: Allen & Unwin, 1980.

Pym, Jim, *Listening to the Light: How to Bring Quaker Simplicity and Integrity into Our Lives*. London: Rider Books, 1999.

————, *What Kind of God, What Kind of Healing*. Oxford: The Spiritual Healing Society, 1999.

Reps, Paul, and Nyogen Senzaki, *Zen Flesh, Zen Bones*. Tokyo: Tuttle, 1963. Also Boston: Shambhala Publications, 1994.

Suzuki, D. T., *Essays in Zen Buddhism* (3 volumes). London: Rider Books, 1992.

————, *Manual of Zen Buddhism*. London: Rider, 1957.

Woodward, F. L., *Some Sayings of the Buddha*. Oxford: Oxford University Press, 1925.

Zuiken, Rev. Saizo Inagaki, *Anjin*. Kyoto: Horai Association, 1988.

————, *Nembutsu and Zen*. Kyoto: Horai Association, 1995.

General Buddhism

Cush, Denise, *Buddhism*. London: Hodder & Stoughton, 1993.

Findly, Ellison Banks, ed., *Women's Buddhism, Buddhism's Women: Tradition, Revision, Renewal*. Boston: Wisdom Publications, 2000.

Fowler, Merv, *Buddhism: Beliefs and Practices*. Brighton: Sussex Academic Press, 1999.

Gethin, Rupert, *The Foundations of Buddhism*. Oxford: Oxford University Press, 1998.

Gombrich, Richard F., *How Buddhism Began: The Conditioned Genesis of the Early Teachings*. London: Athlone Press, 1997.

Harris, Elizabeth, J.,*What Buddhists Believe*. Oxford: Oneworld Publications, 1999.

Humphreys, Christmas, *A Popular Dictionary of Buddhism*. London: Curzon Press, 1998.

Ross, Nancy Wilson, *Buddhism: A Way of Life and Thought.* New York: Random House, 1981.

Zen

Abe, Masao, ed., *A Zen Life: D. T. Suzuki Remembered.* New York: Weatherhill, 1986.

Besserman, Perle and Manfred Steger, *Crazy Clouds, Zen Radicals, Rebels and Reformers.* Boston: Shambhala, 1991.

Franck, Frederick, *Zen Seeing, Zen Drawing: Meditation in Action.* New York: Bantam Books, 1993.

Senzaki, Nyogen, *Like a Dream, Like a Fantasy.* Edited by Eido Shimano Roshi. New York: Japan Publications, 1978.

Suzuki, D. T., *Living by Zen.* Boston: Red Wheel/Weiser, 1972.

Suzuki, Shunryu, *Zen Mind, Beginner's Mind: Informal Talks on Zen Meditation and Practice.* New York: Weatherhill, 1997.

Watts, Alan, *The Wisdom of Insecurity: A Message for an Age of Anxiety.* New York: Random House, 1968.

Pure Land

Suzuki, D. T., *Buddha of Infinite Light: The Teachings of Shin Buddhism, the Japanese Way of Wisdom and Compassion.* Boston: Shambhala Publications, 2002.

Tam, Thich Thien, *Buddhism of Wisdom and Faith, Pure Land Principles and Practice.* Sutra Translation Committee of the United States and Canada, New York and Toronto, 1994.

Unno, Taitetsu, *River of Fire, River of Water: An Introduction to the Pure Land Tradition of Shin Buddhism.* New York: Doubleday, 1998.

Buddhism and Other Faiths

Boorstein, Sylvia, *That's Funny, You Don't Look Buddhist: On Being a Faithful Jew and a Passionate Buddhist*. San Francisco: Harper, 1998.

Borg, Marcus, ed., *Jesus and Buddha: The Parallel Sayings*. Berkeley: Seastone, 1999.

Dalai Lama, *The Good Heart: A Buddhist Perspective on the Teachings of Jesus*. Boston: Wisdom Publications, 1998.

de Mello, Anthony, *One Minute Wisdom*. Image Books, 1988.

————, *Taking Flight: A Book of Story Meditations*. Image Books, 1990.

Franck, Frederick, *A Little Compendium on That Which Matters*. New York: St. Martin's Press, 1993.

Graham, Dom Aelred, *Conversations: Christian and Buddhist*. London: Collins, 1968.

Hanh, Thich Nhat, *Going Home: Jesus and Buddha as Brothers*. New York: Riverhead Books, 2000.

Pym, Jim, *The Pure Principle, Quakers and Other Faith Traditions*. Sessions of York, 2000.

Smith, Bradford, *Meditation: the Inward Art*. London: Allen & Unwin, 1964.

Walker, Susan, ed., *Speaking of Silence: Christians and Buddhists on the Contemplative Way*. Mahwah, NJ: Paulist Press, 1987.

Useful Addresses

✦

General

TRICYCLE: THE BUDDHIST REVIEW

Editorial: 92 Vandam Street, New York, NY 10013; 212-645-1143

Subscriptions: P.O. Box 2077, Marion, OH 43306; 800-873-9871

www.tricycle.com

The best and most up-to-date address for contacts of all Buddhist groups throughout the U.S. is *Tricycle* magazine.

THE AMERICAN BUDDHIST CONGRESS (ABC)

3835 R East Thousand Oaks Boulevard, Suite 450

West Lake Village, CA 91362

877-728-3341

www.americanbuddhistcongress.org

e-mail email@americanbuddhistcongress.org

The ABC is dedicated to promoting Buddhism in the United States, and to developing an "American" Buddhism that combines traditional Asian practices with Western values and vocabulary. The organization sponsors seminars and festivals, maintains a database of speakers and publishes a journal.

THE INSTITUTE FOR WORLD RELIGIONS

c/o the Berkeley Buddhist Monastery
2304 McKinley Avenue, Berkeley, CA 94703
www.drba.org
e-mail paramita@dnai.com

The Institute works to foster understanding between different Buddhist sects, and promotes the study of religious and cultural Asian and Western traditions. They hold seminars, lectures, meditation groups and formal academic classes.

Tibetan Buddhism

There are many Tibetan schools and groups in the U.S. Below are just a few. For others consult the directory at www.tricycle.com.

THE BERKELEY SHAMBHALA CENTER

2288 Fulton Street, Berkeley, CA 94704
510-841-3242
www.shambhala.org/centers/berkeley
e-mail shambhal@pacbell.net

c/o SERGIO AYALA, BUDDHIST CENTER AUSTIN

1507 Northridge Street, Austin, TX 78723
512-420-9388
www.uts.cc.utexas.edu/~diamond
e-mail austin@diamondway-center.org

CAMBRIDGE DZOGCHEN SANGHA

11 Longfellow Park, Cambridge, MA 02138
617-628-1702
www.cambridgedzogchen.org
e-mail mike@cambridgedzogchen.org

Theravada Buddhism

There are a number of Theravada groups throughout the U.S., with emphasis on Sri Lankan and Thai traditions. For details consult the directory at www.tricycle.com.

Pure Land Buddhism

BUDDHIST CHURCHES OF AMERICA HEADQUARTERS (BCA)

1710 Octavia Street, San Francisco, CA 94109
415-776-5600
e-mail bcahq@pacbell.net

The BCA practices only Pure Land Buddhism, and maintains a bookstore with religious texts. They are a good resource for any inquiries into the Pure Land sect.

Soto Zen

There are many Soto Zen groups in the U.S. The address given below is just one suggestion.

SHASTA ABBEY

3724 Summit Drive, Mt. Shasta, CA 96067
530-926-4208
www.shastaabbey.org
e-mail guestmaster@shastaabbey.org

Rinzai Zen

There are a number of Rinzai Zen groups in the U.S. Each is under the direction of a different teacher. For information consult the directory at www.tricycle.com.

Other Seastone/Ulysses Press Titles

✦

BEFORE HE WAS BUDDHA: THE LIFE OF SIDDHARTHA
Hammalawa Saddhatissa   Introduction by Jack Kornfield, $12.00

Written in a lucid, flowing style, this biographical profile reveals the strength and gentleness of Buddha's character and brings to life the compassion that gave his teachings universal appeal.

EINSTEIN AND BUDDHA: THE PARALLEL SAYINGS
Thomas J. McFarlane   Introduction by Wes Nisker, $19.00

Provocative and insightful, this book demonstrates the parallels between Western thought and Eastern religion and what they communicate about the deep common ground of scientific and spiritual truth. Hardback.

HOW MEDITATION HEALS: A SCIENTIFIC EXPLANATION
Eric Harrison, $12.95

In straightforward, practical terms, *How Meditation Heals* reveals how and why meditation improves the natural functioning of the human body.

HOW TO MEDITATE: AN ILLUSTRATED GUIDE
TO CALMING THE MIND AND RELAXING THE BODY
Paul Roland, $16.95

Offers a friendly, illustrated approach to calming the mind and raising consciousness through various techniques, including basic meditation, visualization, body scanning for tension, affirmations and mantras.

JESUS AND BUDDHA: THE PARALLEL SAYINGS
Marcus Borg, Editor   Introduction by Jack Kornfield, $14.00

Traces the life stories and beliefs of Jesus and Buddha, then presents a comprehensive collection of their remarkably similar teachings on facing pages.

JESUS AND LAO TZU: THE PARALLEL SAYINGS
Martin Aronson   Introduction by David Steindl-Rast, $19.00

Comparing the New Testament with the Tao Te Ching, Taoism's most sacred book, *Jesus and Lao Tzu* features an astonishing series of examples in which these two spiritual masters lead their followers down the same path in spite of differences in time and geography. Hardback.

JESUS AND MOSES: THE PARALLEL SAYINGS
Joey Green   Introduction by Stewart Vogel, $19.00

Jesus and Moses presents the sayings of Jesus and the parallel teachings of Judaism found in the Old Testament, Talmud and other Jewish works. Hardback.

MUSIC OF SILENCE
David Steindl-Rast with Sharon Lebell   Introduction by Kathleen Norris, $12.00

A noted Benedictine monk shows us how to incorporate the sacred meaning of monastic life into our everyday world by paying attention to the "seasons of the day" and the enlivening messages to be found in each moment.

PILATES WORKBOOK: ILLUSTRATED STEP-BY-STEP GUIDE TO MATWORK TECHNIQUES
Michael King, $12.95

Illustrates the core matwork movements exactly as Joseph Pilates intended them to be performed; readers learn each movement by simply following the photographic sequences and explanatory captions.

TEACH YOURSELF TO MEDITATE IN 10 SIMPLE LESSONS: DISCOVER RELAXATION AND CLARITY OF MIND IN JUST MINUTES A DAY
Eric Harrison, $12.95

Guides the reader through ten easy-to-follow core meditations. Also includes practical and enjoyable "spot meditations" that require only a few minutes a day and can be incorporated into the busiest of schedules.

WHAT WOULD BUDDHA DO?: 101 ANSWERS TO LIFE'S DAILY DILEMMAS
Franz Metcalf, $9.95

Much as the "WWJD?" books help Christians live better lives by drawing on the wisdom of Jesus, this "WWBD?" book provides advice on improving your life by following the wisdom of another great teacher—Buddha.

WHAT WOULD BUDDHA DO AT WORK?: 101 ANSWERS TO WORKPLACE DILEMMAS
Franz Metcalf and BJ Gallagher Hateley, $16.95

What Would Buddha Do at Work? uses the gentle teachings of Buddha to help people discover deeper meaning in their work lives. Hardback.

YOGA IN FOCUS: POSTURES, SEQUENCES AND MEDITATIONS
Jessie Chapman   Photographs by Dhyan, $14.95

A yoga book unlike any other, *Yoga In Focus* could just as easily be a gift book as a tutorial. The presentation captures the very essence of yoga, combining perfectly positioned figures in meditative black-and-white photos.

To order these books call 800-377-2542 or 510-601-8301, fax 510-601-8307, e-mail ulysses@ulyssespress.com, or write to Ulysses Press, P.O. Box 3440, Berkeley, CA 94703. All retail orders are shipped free of charge. California residents must include sales tax. Allow two to three weeks for delivery.

About the Author

✦

JIM PYM was born and brought up a Roman Catholic, and has had a lifelong interest in religion and spirituality. He became a Buddhist through hearing a monk lecture on the *Kalama Sutra*, in which the Buddha tells us only to believe what is true and helpful for us. This has been the key to his spiritual journey.

Since then, he has experienced many aspects of Buddhism, from Theravadin to Tibetan, and from Zen to Pure Land. He is currently the coordinator for the Pure Land Buddhist Fellowship, editor of their journal, *Pure Land Notes*, and a member of the Council of the Buddhist Society, London. Jim is also a member of the Religious Society of Friends (Quakers), and a member of a Buddhist–Christian dialogue group, which has met for more than ten years. He firmly believes that there is one thing better than being either a Buddhist or a Christian, and that is to be both, and feels that Buddhism must take account of Western culture if it is to become fully established in the West.

Among his other interests are interfaith work, spiritual healing and jazz and folk music. He is currently studying for an MA in Religious Experience with the University of Wales in Lampeter. He also teaches meditation, and is active in leading retreats and workshops.

Jim's other books include *Listening to the Light* (Rider Books) on Quaker spirituality, and *The Pure Principle* (Sessions of York) on Quakers and world faiths.